Praying God
blesses you abundantly
as you dig into His word!
Anastasia Corbin
Zephaniah 3:17

WHEN THE BASES ARE LOADED

Natalie Replogle
Anastasia Corbin

Blessings to you!
♡ Natalie Replogle

D0841437

Cover photography by Darcy Holsopple Photography. (www.darcyholsopplephotography.com)

Published by White Feather Press. (www.whitefeatherpress.com)

ISBN 978-1-61808-140-7

Printed in the United States of America

White Feather Press

Reafferming Faith in God, Family and Country

NATALIE

To my mom, Sue Cripe. All I ever wanted to be when I grew up was a mom, and that's because of you. You are the most caring, thoughtful, and giving woman I know. You have been my rock and biggest cheerleader my entire life, the greatest example of pursing Jesus during the ups and downs of life, and the best role model of what a loving and devoted mom looks like. Most importantly, thank you for teaching me at a young age about Jesus. It's the most valuable gift I will ever be given. I love you!

ANASTASIA

To my hero and adopted Dad, Don Schweingruber. Thank you for taking time to listen, encourage and pour into me. I would not be who I am without your love and influence. Until we meet again…

THE
ULTIMATE
SACRIFICE

"But he was pierced for our transgressions, he was crushed for our iniquities; the punishment that brought us peace was on him, and by his wounds we are healed."

Isaiah 53:5

As I reflect on the great sacrifice Christ made for us, I am humbled by the fact He would have died on that cross even if it was only for me. Jesus would have done it just for one. That is how incredibly loved we are.

The Messiah came to be tortured because He knew we couldn't save ourselves. The Messiah willingly went up on the cross to free us from death and our sins. The Messiah allowed that punishment to be put on Him so that we could have eternal life and make our home in Heaven. By that great sacrifice, the Messiah has cleansed us and forgiven us by His grace.

You are that important, that cherished, that God would have sent his Son to earth to be persecuted, rejected, and die for your sins alone. Take a moment to let that pour over you. Let it sink into every nook and cranny of your heart, every part that has a hole, or crack, or barrier. Jesus would have done it all, just for you! No matter where you are in life, grab hold of this truth… Jesus loves YOU. Jesus came to rescue YOU. Jesus died for YOU. Jesus saved YOU.

As a mom, I hurt when my children hurt. There are so many

times I wish I could take their pain or sickness upon myself. That is what God wants to do for you. That is the gift He wants to give you, if you are willing to receive it. He sees you and wants you to lay everything down at His feet. He's already made the grand sacrifice, now it's just up to you to allow Him to take it. There is such freedom in giving your life over to Christ. Jesus tells us in Matthew 7:13–14 "Enter through the narrow gate. For wide is the gate and broad is the road that leads to destruction, and many enter through it. But small is the gate and narrow the road that leads to life, and only a few find it."

Jesus is that small gate and narrow road. All He asks is that you accept Him and ask Him to come into your heart. If you have yet to do that, He is ready and waiting for you with open arms.

Heavenly Father, thank You for loving me so much that you sent Your only to Son to bear my sins and die for me so that I may spend eternity in Heaven. In Your Word, you tell me that for the wages of sin is death, but the gift of God is eternal life in Christ Jesus our LORD (Romans 6:23). Thank You for Your gift and what a treasure it is to find You and follow after You. Make Your home in my heart. In Jesus name, Amen.

—Natalie

Today God is stirring my heart by…

DWELL

"Let the word of Christ dwell in you richly."

Colossians 3:16

The Bible is one of the greatest books. It has been around for a very long time. It has been on best sellers' lists and said to be the most sold book of all time. The Bible is a love letter from God to His children. God uses the Word to challenge, convict, and comfort us. It's a powerful book. Are you taking time each day in God's Word? Do you listen for God to speak to you?

I LOVE to spend time in God's word! My life has been literally changed because of time spent in it. It hasn't always been easy or fun to make time for the Word. It's been a journey over many years.

I remember in college when I first became a Christian learning that I could have a Bible of my own. I remembered being amazed by that fact. My journey of reading the Bible began at that time in my life. I picked up a study Bible and a devotional to help me learn about the Bible. It was a process but I also tried to keep reading it.

In our early years of marriage, my husband and I read through the Bible in a year. As I kept reading daily, I kept learning. But, I also had the mornings where I would fall asleep or read the Bible and not understand anything I just read. My husband challenged me to keep reading and asking the Holy Spirit for guidance. He encouraged me to pray for a hunger for God's word. That was a life changing prayer for me. Ever since those years, I have continued to pray for a hunger for God's word. My prayer now is that God will expand my appetite for His Word—and oh my, He is answering that prayer!

How about you? How is your time in God's word? Are you getting into it daily? If you're in a spot where it's dry and you don't feel like you're getting into the Bible when you read, don't give up! Keep reading the Bible daily. Find someone to hold you accountable. Surround yourself with people who are passionate about God's word. Pray each day for a fresh hunger for God's word. It will take time to come but soon you won't be able to get enough of it. Ask God to give you that hunger for His word. Friends, I promise you that He will!

Heavenly Father, please teach me what it means to dwell in Your Word. Please show me how to make time in Your Word a priority. God, I want to desire Your words more than my daily bread. Would You please fill me with a fresh hunger for Your Word? Thank You LORD. In Jesus name, Amen.

—Anastasia

Today God is stirring my heart by…

THE MANY HATS YOU WEAR

"He gives strength to the weary and increases the power of the weak. Even youths grow tired and weary, and young men stumble and fall; but those who hope in the LORD will renew their strength. They will soar on wings like eagles; they will run and not grow weary, they will walk and not be faint."

Isaiah 40: 29–31

There are some days as a mom, I really just want to go lock myself in my bathroom and go to my happy place. The place where there are no dishes to wash, no siblings fighting, no clothes to fold, no mouths to feed or bottoms that need to be wiped, and it is quiet—very, very quiet! I'll be honest, there are days where I just want to throw my hands up in the air and scream (and there are days that I really do).

As moms, we are pulled into so many directions and wear many hats. We are a chef, referee, accountant, seamstress, chauffer, principal, judge, cleaner, mentor, party planner, CEO of our household, maid, shepherd, etc.—all the while trying to keep a smile our face, serve our husband and children and just try not to lose it. Some of these hats fit perfectly and you wear them with pride, others are not the color you look good in, but you are forced to wear them anyway. We deal, we cope, and we keep moving.

So how do we not only survive, but thrive as a mom? We go to our Creator for help. A lot of times I notice when I am struggling it's because I am trying to do everything myself or in my control. But when I take the time to spend with the LORD, asking for His strength and His mindset, life isn't as overwhelming. The obstacles don't feel as high, the chores don't feel so mundane, and I am reminded the good I am doing.

Paul tells us how to find this strength. In Ephesians 3:16, he says, "I pray that out of His glorious riches He may strengthen you with power through His Spirit in your inner being." It doesn't start by changing the circumstances around us, but by changing our heart— our spirit and inner being! God wants to help you flourish and thrive as a mom. He wants to see you walk in peace and prosperity. He desires to help you and strengthen you to be the best mom He has created you to be… He's just waiting for you to ask!

Heavenly Father, being a mom is such a great privilege and I never want to take it for granted. Help me today, and the days to come, to serve You as I serve my family. Renew my strength as I strive daily to greater Your Kingdom. In Jesus name, Amen.

—Natalie

Today God is stirring my heart by…

HOLDING TIGHT

"I cling to you; your strong right hand holds me securely."

Psalm 63:8

"Look at those waves!! They are huge!!" exclaimed our four kids as they jumped up and down. The waves quickly washed up any creation in the sand. As they thundered in, the waves looked like mountains compared to some of my kids.

This summer, we spent time on Lake Michigan for our family vacation. On this particular morning, we stood amazed at the power of the waves. The younger two kids tentatively put their feet in the water and that was enough for them. They quickly busied themselves with playing in the sand. The older two kids ventured out a little farther, but not much. I soaked it all in and enjoyed my spot on the sand.

As soon as my husband went in the water, the older kids grabbed hold of his hand and stepped out a little further into the waves. I watched my kids get a little taller as they held on to Daddy. They ventured out farther and farther. As the waves came at them they held tight to Daddy's hand. As I watched, I felt the scare in my kids, watched the hold get tighter, and then relax some when they realized Daddy wasn't going to let them get hurt. After this realization, they had so much fun in the waves. Think about all that they would have missed if they had given into their scare. I am so glad they trusted their Daddy. Soon after this, I loved watching my younger two kids step out a little more into the water. Analiah and Caleb watched their older siblings trust Daddy, so they knew they could too.

As I sat there soaking this all in, God whispered to my heart; "Will you take a step into the ragging waves? Will you trust me like your kids are trusting their Dad? Will you hold tight to my hand and relax because I have everything under control? I won't let you get hurt my daughter. I will take care of you."

As I listened to the voice of my Heavenly Daddy, tears streamed down my face. God has proven faithful again and again. How could I not trust Him in the waves of life? Why wouldn't I take God's hand and hold tight? I resolved in that moment to take my Daddy's hand and hold tight no matter what size the waves of life would be. In the hard times and the good times. And I resolved to relax in God's embrace because He will take care of me.

How about you? Are you holding tight to your Daddy's hand when the waves of life come at you?

Heavenly Father, thank You for holding out Your hand to me. I love that I can grab hold any time that I am fearful. The waves of life will come, in fact right now, I am facing some tough ones. But, God You are bigger than those waves. Please help me to trust You. Help me to relax in Your embrace. Thank You Jesus. I love You, LORD. In Jesus name, Amen.

—Anastasia

Today God is stirring my heart by...

CODE BLUE

"I, even I, am He who blots out your transgressions, for my own sake, and remembers your sins no more."

Isaiah 43:25

Five years ago I lost my son, Brayden, at the grocery store. It was unfortunately the really bad kind where the doors became locked and all shoppers heard this over the speakers: "Code Blue! Code Blue! Attention all Wal-Mart Associates, we are in lockdown. We have a missing child. Boy, age 4, blond hair, red shirt, navy shorts." Yep. I know. Mom of the year award right here! I would have dressed up for the occasion had I known. In case you're wondering, Brayden thought it would be fun to play hide and seek with me...but forgot the slight detail of telling me he was playing this game. And boy did he play the game well. We (as in myself and the surrounding employees and managers)—enter face palm here—finally found him down an aisle tucked behind some boxes. Brayden, of course, has *never* let me forget it. To this day, when we drive into the parking lot, without fail, he says, "Hey mom, remember when you lost me here?"

This situation reminds me of our road to forgiveness, or more so, *what it is not*. I don't know about you, but I am so thankful that I serve the God Almighty that doesn't hold my sins against me. The God of the Universe that doesn't continue to remind me of the times I've fallen short. The King of Kings that once I ask for forgiveness, that's it. It's forgiven... forgotten! King David spoke of this truth in Psalm 51:7 after he committed adultery. "Cleanse me with hyssop and I will be clean; wash me, and I will be whiter than snow." Hyssop branches were used by the Israelites to place the blood of the lamb over their doors ways. This act saved them from death and secured their release from slavery. When we ask for forgiveness, it not only cleanses our hearts and repairs the separation we made with God, but it also releases us from the sin that keeps us in slavery. It makes us pure again, without blemish.

Is there a sin that you are holding on to? Give it to God so He can break your chains and give you freedom!

Heavenly Father, bring to light the sin(s) that keep me captive, that keep me from drawing closer to you. Thank You for sending Your Son to come and save me from my sins, and that those sins are forever forgotten. In Jesus name, Amen.

—Natalie

Today God is stirring my heart by…

GOD CARES

"And even the very hairs of your head are all numbered.
So don't be afraid; you are worth more than many
sparrows."

Matthew 10:30–31

Baby ducks, an egg shell in cookie dough, missing books and movie, a clay flower in the freezer. These are all very little and random things. You may wonder why I am even making this list. This list reminds me that God cares about the little things.

Over the past several months I have taken note of the way God has provided and answered some prayers. It has been so fun to be on the lookout. My oldest daughter, Micaela, loves creating things. One day she created a flower out of molding clay. Micaela proudly placed it in the freezer to harden. A few days later she investigated and found her flower was missing. Micaela came up to me and asked "Mom, where is my flower?" I helped her look high and low to no avail. We then prayed about finding it. I assured her that God cared about her creation and wanted to help her find it. A few days later, I opened the refrigerator to pull out some ketchup and found Micaela's flower creation resting on top of the condiments. She was ecstatic! It was a great teaching moment. God does cares about the little things.

Here are a few other examples from the last couple months. My kids love going to the library. Each week they pick out books and movies. One week, we could not find a missing book. In fact we had received the slip saying it was overdue. We searched high and low, retraced all the steps, etc. but still could not find it. So, the kids and I prayed and asked God to show us. A day or two later, I was cleaning in the girls bedroom and the thought came to mind to look under the bunk bed. And there tucked far in the back corner was the missing book. Later I found the movie we lost hiding under our downstairs couch. God cares about the little things.

I made cookies the other day, I knew I had dropped an egg shell somewhere in the batter but could not find it. So, I prayed about it and finished making the batter. As I was about to scoop out the cookies to bake, I found the egg shell. God cares about the little things.

A few weeks ago, we headed to the duck farm with friends to pick up some duck eggs. My 2 and 4 year old were really hoping to see baby ducks but I told them we probably wouldn't. On our way out, a lady who worked there noticed all the kids and directed us to someone who could take us to see the baby ducks. Our kids were beyond thrilled! Before a prayer was even uttered, God answered it and we saw baby ducks that morning. God cares about the little things. Our key verse for today communicates this truth also. God knows everything and He cares for you.

The list goes on and on. And continues to grow each day. What have you noticed? What ways do you see God caring about the little things in your life? Be on the lookout.

Heavenly Father, thank You for caring about the little things. I love the ways you have provided and answered so many prayers. It has been so fun to be on the lookout. I will keep looking for Your faithfulness. In Jesus name, Amen.

—Anastasia

Today God is stirring my heart by…

SALT OF
THE EARTH

"You are the salt of the earth. But if the salt loses its saltiness, how can it be made salty again? It is no longer good for anything, except to be thrown out and trampled by men. You are the light of the world. A city on a hill cannot be hidden. Neither do people light a lamp and put it under a bowl. Instead they put it on its stand, and it gives light to everyone in the house. In the same way, let your light shine before men, that they may see your good deeds and praise your Father in heaven."

Matthew 5:13–16

I only have a couple pet-peeves in life, and one of them revolves around my cooking. My husband has learned the hard way and very quickly about this one that can sometimes really bother me. Drum roll please, because I know you're waiting on the edge of your seats… it's when people salt the food I've prepared *before* tasting it. Now please understand me, I don't care at all if people salt my food, but for heaven's sake, just try it first!

Yes, there is a point, and here it is… So let's say you have salt in your salt shaker, but it has lost its taste, what does that mean? If seasoning has lost its flavor, it has no value. Which, you would be fine at my dinner table because my food is (cough-cough) perfect. But in life, Jesus is saying if we make no effort to change the world around us or further God's Kingdom, then we are *useless* to Him. It may be harsh to hear, but it's the truth.

The scripture above tells us how we are to be the salt of the earth. We as believers should have an aroma about us that stands out. That someone shouldn't have to get to know us to find out if we are believers, but the fruits of the Spirit radiate off us. That when people meet us they immediately know something is different by the way we speak, the way we serve, and the undeniable joy that fills us. Our spiritual scent should draw others in and makes them think, "How can I get what she has?"

We are also to let our light shine before men. In order to do that, we need to get out into the world and point people to Jesus. That might mean we need to be bold when we speak, stand firm in our morals and values, share what God has done in our life, and walk a righteous life.

Just as seasoning brings out the best in our food, we should bring the best out in others. Salt doesn't blend into our food, it makes it better! Don't blend into the world around you, stand out and make a difference!

Heavenly Father, I want to make a difference for You and Your Kingdom. Give me the power to make the changes I need to make. Give me the courage to stand out and give value to Your name. May others find You by watching me serve and praise You. In Jesus name, Amen.

—Natalie

Today God is stirring my heart by...

STRONG TOWER

"The name of the LORD is a strong tower; the righteous run to it and are safe."

Proverbs 18:10

Who or what have you been running to when things are hard? Where do you go for strength when you are weary? Where do you go to feel safe? We all turn to someone or something when things get tough. I would like to suggest that you turn to the only One who can truly satisfy. The only One who can meet all your needs—Jesus. His name is a STRONG tower.

As I read this verse, I wondered about the structure of a tower. How do we know it's strong? I also wondered how it is used. So, I did a little research to find out how God is like a strong tower. The definition of a tower is "such a structure used or intended for a stronghold or fortress." Towers are built taller than they are wide. Towers are self-supporting structures. Three things really stood out to me from my research. Fortress, stronghold and advantage.

First, I found that a strong tower is a fortress which is a place of security. In God, you are always safe. There is never a doubt that He will protect you. When we are afraid or worried about a situation, the best thing to do is run to God. Run to your place of security.

A strong tower is also stronghold for you. A stronghold is a well-fortified place. This place helps protect or strengthen you against an attack. God is always there to protect you from whatever comes your way. He will strengthen you in every way for the battles you face. The key is depending on God instead of yourself. When you find yourself in a battle, please run to God.

Finally, a strong tower is an advantage. Towers were built taller than they are wide. So, when you are at the top of the tower, you have a big advantage. You have a great view of the surrounding areas and the battle. Another advantage is seeing the enemy. All of this is to your advantage because you can help your side defeat the enemy with this knowledge. You can help them know the plan of attack.

God, our strong tower, is an advantage. He already has defeated the enemy so we have power in His name. God gives you a clear plan of attack to battle the enemy each day. In Ephesians 6, God encourages us to put on our armor daily. He sets you up for success in the battles of life.

God also can see all the surrounding area, the bigger picture of our lives. He knows that if He would give all of that to us, we couldn't handle it. We need to take the time daily to be in His word and communicating with God, our strong tower. Through this daily communication, we will get to know God more. Our desires will also become His desires for our lives.

God is our fortress and stronghold. In Him, we do have the advantage. Run to your Strong Tower today.

Heavenly Father, thank You for being my Strong Tower. Thank You that I can run to You at any time throughout my day. Please help me to trust You. You know the big picture and I can rest in that truth. I love you LORD. In Jesus name, Amen.

—Anastasia

Today God is stirring my heart by...

KEEP LOOKING UP

"Therefore, my dear brothers, stand firm. Let nothing move you. Always give yourselves fully to the work of the LORD, because you know that your labor in the LORD is not in vain."

1 Corinthians 15:58

This past summer my husband and I taught two of our children how to ride a bike. Every parent that has helped a child learn to ride a bike understands the back pain involved in teaching this skill. We had that, times two. For hours at a time you would find us hunched behind their bike, running up and down our street behind them. I'm happy to tell you that I have finally been able to stand straight again. When helping them, I felt like my words were a broken record of, "Keep pedaling!" and "Look up!" We noticed as they rode, every time they put their head down to focus on how they were riding, they would slow down and immediately begin to tip.

I began to realize how often we can fall into the same pattern spiritually. So often when our attention turns to our problems or the circumstances that surround us, we begin to falter in our walk and we lose where our focus should be. It says in Colossians 3:1–2, "Since, then, you have been raised with Christ, set your hearts on things above, where Christ is seated at the right hand of God. Set your minds on things above, not on earthly things."

A few things happen when our focus in misplaced. We miss out on seeing God's goodness and the beauty of what He is doing around us and in us. When my kids would look down while riding, they missed so much. They missed the entire view before them. They missed anything dangerous they needed to look out for. They missed how far they had gone and the progress they had made.

Another thing that happens when our focus is misplaced is that we begin to forget why we are here and that this is not our home. God reminds us in 2 Corinthians 4:16–18, "Therefore we do not lose heart. Though outwardly we are wasting away, yet inwardly we are being renewed day by day. For our light and momentary troubles are achieving for us an eternal glory that far outweighs them all. So we fix our eyes not on what is seen, but on what is unseen. For what is seen is temporary, but what is unseen is eternal." God has promised us that He is preparing a place for us. That all of our sorrow, heartache, hard work, wise choices, obedience, faithful pursuit to become a woman after God's own heart, will NOT return void. Often times we can get frustrated because we aren't seeing the results we want, but we can rest assure that nothing we do is in vain. We are not living to make this life easy, but to prepare ourselves for our eternal home.

A question to ask is, "Am I living for earthly gain or heavenly gain?"

Heavenly Father, may I fix my eyes on You. Remind me each day not to become weary in doing good, for at the proper time I will reap a harvest if I don't give up. (Galatians 6:9) Help me not to be discouraged, but to trust you for the results. In Jesus name, Amen.

—Natalie

Today God is stirring my heart by…

GINGERBREAD COOKIE

"This is how much God loved the world: He gave his Son, his one and only Son. And this is why: so that no one need be destroyed; by believing in him, anyone can have a whole and lasting life. God didn't go to all the trouble of sending his Son merely to point an accusing finger, telling the world how bad it was. He came to help, to put the world right again."

John 3:16–17

"My cookie is broken" pouted Caleb, our 3 year old son. He held up his gingerbread cookie and showed my husband and me. We were at our older daughter's school for a Christmas luncheon. The dessert was iced gingerbread man cookies. The leg of Caleb's cookie was broken and he was very sad. I offered to switch my whole cookie with his. Caleb instantly lit up and happily traded with me. All was right in his world.

After taking the cookie from Caleb, I looked it over. There was a clear break in the leg and crumbs littered the package. Jesus whispered to my heart in that moment. "I have taken your brokenness and made you whole again. I gave my life so that you could have eternal life." In the middle of a school cafeteria, I was once again reminded of how much I am loved by the Creator of the Universe.

The Creator of the Universe loves you too. Jesus has done the same for you dear one. My question for you is have you let Him take your brokenness and make you whole again? Have you made Jesus the LORD of your life so that you can spend eternity with Him in heaven?

In our key verses for today, God's word is very clear. He sent His son Jesus so that anyone could have whole and lasting life. We must receive this free gift and ask Jesus to be the LORD of our lives. It is that simple.

When Jesus steps into our lives, He brings wholeness and healing. Jesus changes us from deep within. We need to continually walk in this wholeness no matter what comes our way.

Too often we stay broken. We get caught up in patterns that are unhealthy and don't even realize it. The patterns become normal to us. I have learned to come before Jesus each day and ask Him to reveal to me what lies I am believing. I also ask Jesus to show me what in my character is not lining up with His character. Where do I need to make some changes? God is so faithful to show me one step at a time. He cares more about change in my life than I even do. God longs for me to be more like Jesus even more than I do. Amazing, right?

The God of the Universe cares very deeply about you too. He desires for you to become more like His son Jesus. Will you bring Jesus your brokenness and let Him fix you? Will you let God make you whole again? God doesn't want you to walk in brokenness but in wholeness in Him. God wants freedom for you.

Heavenly Father, thank You for sending Your only Son Jesus to earth so that I may have eternal life. Thank You for taking my brokenness and making me whole again. Help me to continually give my brokenness to You each day and let you heal me. God, please help me to be in Your Word each day. It brings life, truth and guides me in Your ways. I love You, LORD. In Jesus name, Amen.

—Anastasia

Today God is stirring my heart by…

MILK
AND HONEY

"The heart of the righteous weighs its answers, but the mouth of the wicked gushes evil."

Proverbs 15:28

On certain days, by the end of the day my nerves are frayed and my patience is on a short leash. And in order for me to relax, what has to come first? That's right, the children's bedtime routine. Some nights it goes well, other nights I'm ready to pack my bags and run away like my ten-year-old threatened to do on a daily basis when he was younger. One night I had gone into my son's room for the umpteenth time and everything in me wanted to throw a temper tantrum like the ones I had to defuse throughout the day. Instead, I'm pretty sure the Holy Spirit took control and I went in calm with a smile pressed on my face. I rubbed his back, talked with him and gave him more hugs and kisses while informing him that I wouldn't be coming back in. When I started to leave he said, "Mommy, I love your voice. It is so nice and makes me feel good."

I wish I could testify that my voice always sounds like milk and honey toward my children, but sadly this was a rare example. So often I find myself so concerned about the words that I say that I forget about the tone I use. Not only can our words crush our children's spirit, but the tone we use can be just as damaging. In Proverbs 18:21 it says, "The tongue has the power of life and death, and those who love it will eat its fruit." The words I speak to them may be true and what they need to hear, but my harsh tone has just killed any progress I am trying to make. It becomes the example of Proverbs 15:1—"A gentle answer turns away wrath, but a harsh word stirs up anger."

We as moms have a great opportunity to make our home a haven, and that can start by creating moments and conversations that help our children feel safe to share with us. We need our children to hear the truth, but through a respectful response that doesn't crush their spirit. I want my voice to be soothing to their soul and bring life instead of death.

Heavenly Father, guide me each moment to hold my tongue in response until I am able to speak in a loving way. Let my words instill peace upon my children, my husband and those around me. May my tongue produce life not death. In Jesus name, Amen.

— Natalie

Today God is stirring my heart by…

WHAT DO YOU BELIEVE?

"You are precious and honored in my sight, and I love you."

Isaiah 43:4

How would you respond if someone asked you what you believe about yourself? What is the script you have running through your head about your worth? The other day my eyes were opened to what our son was thinking about himself.

During the Christmas season, we have an advent log with a candle for each week of advent. At dinner time is when we typically light the candles. The kids love to take turns blowing out the candles. This year we have added in lighting the candles too. We came up with a new system so it's fair for all involved.

During the week, Nathan, our oldest son was home from school due to being sick the afternoon before. We decided to light the candles at lunch. Nathan really wanted to light the candles and have the girls blow out them out. He wanted to make sure it was fair. My youngest son, Caleb who is 3 years old, piped up, "Micaela is not here so she can't blow them out." Nathan responded "Oh yeah, stupid me!" I thought to myself "What did he just say? I must have heard him wrong." So, I asked Nathan to repeat himself. He responded with the same thing "Stupid me, I forgot Micaela was in school." I tried to stay calm while asking Nathan where he heard that expression from and why was he saying it. Inside my heart was breaking. Why did my son just call himself stupid? Nathan replied "Some kids say that at school, Mom." I responded to Nathan and assured him that he was not stupid.

Next, we talked about the importance of speaking the truth about ourselves. Yes, we make stupid choices but that doesn't define our character. God sees us as special and valuable as stated in our key verse for today. I encouraged Nathan to speak about himself in a way that builds up instead of tears down.

While speaking to Nathan, the Holy Spirit nudged me and asked me if I believed the same thing. How often do I call myself stupid? How often do I speak down to myself and believe the enemies lies? Much too often. In that moment, I was convicted and challenged. I want to talk about myself in a way that builds myself up instead of tears me down. I am a daughter of the King of Kings. I need to hold my head up high and walk like I believe it.

How about you? Do you speak in a way that builds yourself up or in a way that tears yourself down? Take some time today to write down what you say out loud and inside your head about who you are. At the end of the day, ask God to speak the truth over you. Search His word for verses that speak to your true worth.

Heavenly Father, thank You for creating me exactly how You wanted to. Thank You that I am valuable and precious in Your sight. As I go about my day today, help me to think and speak the truth about how valuable I am. You are my Daddy, so that makes me royalty. Please help me to walk in that truth today. In Jesus name, Amen.

—Anastasia

Today God is stirring my heart by…

MARCH
AROUND THE CITY

"Then the Lord said to Joshua, "See, I have delivered Jericho into your hands along with its king and its fighting men. March around the city once with all the armed men. Do this for six days. Have seven priests carry trumpets of rams' horns in front of the ark. On the seventh day, march around the city seven times, with the priests blowing the trumpets. When you hear them sound a long blast on the trumpets, have all the people give a loud shout; then the wall of the city will collapse and the people will go up, every man straight in." Joshua then commanded the people, "Do not give a war cry, do not raise your voices, do not say a word until the day I tell you to shout. Then shout! So he had the ark of the Lord carried around the city, circling it once. Then the people returned to camp and spent the night there."

Joshua 6: 2–5, 10–11

This is a small excerpt from the story of Joshua and the battle of Jericho. I have read this passage many times, but recently I was reading this story to my kids and I viewed it a little differently. I always looked at this story for the fight. How God can help us do anything with His power. How it's a symbol because they were going up against a defeated enemy and we go up against a defeated enemy daily. God had told Joshua beforehand that Jericho was already delivered into his hands. He went into the battle knowing he would win. God has told us the same thing.

But this time something new stuck out to me. The Israelites just didn't immediately go in and attack. They had to wait. For six days they had to march around the city—and then wait. With no other instructions but to march, be quiet, and wait. Isn't it so hard to wait? They knew God had bigger things in store for them, but they had to wait. They knew the victory was theirs, but they had to wait for it. Through their waiting they had to show their faithfulness and follow what God was asking them to do now.

I look back when I had three very young kids and all I felt like I did was change diapers, nurse, discipline, talk about the alphabet, make animal noises, and never sleep—kind of like marching around a city over and over again! This can be the same in all different seasons and experiences we go through in our lives. A job, a family situation, babies to teenagers, decisions, a dream—as you walk around that city day in and day out, I encourage you to stay faithful to what God has called you to do now. Everything we go through is a stepping stone to prepare us for what God has in store for us next. Take time today to rest in the words of Psalm 130:5 "I wait for the LORD, my soul waits, and in his word I put my hope."

Heavenly Father, You have promised in Your Word that in all things You work for the good of those who love You, who have been called according to Your purpose. I love You, Jesus and I want my life to be used by You and for You! During the times when I am waiting on You, help me to be faithful and obedient. In Jesus name, Amen.

—Natalie

Today God is stirring my heart by…

MY
SUSTAINER

"Surely God is my help; the LORD is the one who sustains me."

Psalm 54:4

Can you think of a time that someone helped you? I mean really helped you. They took time out of their very busy life to pour into yours. They helped you solve a big problem or they spent time listening to you share about something on your heart. There are probably many stories you could share about someone who has helped you. I love that we can have people like that in our lives.

Do you know what I love even more than that? That the King of Kings and Creator of the Whole Universe helps us. That God cares so deeply about us that He is involved personally in our lives. In our key verse it states that surely God is our help. He is the one who sustains us. What does it mean to sustain? The definition of sustain is "to support, hold, or bear the weight of." Let's put that in our verse: The LORD is the one who supports, holds and bears the weight of us.

God supports us. He is always there to help us with any problem. God is there when we are happy and He is there when we are sad. Whatever emotion or situation we are facing in our day, God is there to support us. He fills us with strength and joy. He gives us His peace. God supports us.

God also holds us. God cares very deeply about what is on our heart. He brings great comfort as we spend time with Him. In 2 Corinthians 7:6a it says, "But God, who comforts the downcast." What a promise! In Psalm 34:18, we read "The LORD is close to the brokenhearted and saves those who are crushed in spirit." God is close to you. He uses people to give us tangible hugs. God loves to hold His children.

God bears the weight of our burdens. This just amazes me. The King of Kings and LORD of LORDs bears the weight of my burdens. Why? Just because He is God and He loves me. God does the same for you. The key here is that we need to hand over the burdens. Too often we try to carry them on our own strength. We get tired, worn out and wonder why we are struggling. This is when we need to take a step back and see if we are carrying our burdens or if God is. I promise you that you will feel lighter and better when you give your burdens to Jesus.

God is surely our help. God longs to support you and hold you close. God wants to bear the weight of your burdens. Will you hand them over to Him today? Will you let God help and support you?

Heavenly Father, I stand in awe of You. You have so many people to pay attention to in this world, yet You care so deeply about everything I am going through. Thank You. You long to carry my burdens. Please help me to hand them over and let You help me. Thank You for supporting and holding me. I love You, LORD. In Jesus name, Amen.

—Anastasia

Today God is stirring my heart by…

WATCH OUT
FOR THE
HAIR DRYER

"Watch and pray so that you will not fall into temptation. The spirit is willing, but the body is weak."

Matthew 26:41

Many years ago my husband Greg was out mowing the yard when he came across my hair-dryer. Yep, you read that correctly. It was just outside laying in the middle of the grass. To this day I have no idea how it got there. Well, I have no idea how it got there, but I have a pretty good idea who did it. It wasn't my husband. It wasn't me. I am quite confident it wasn't the baby or the dog. So that leaves an adorable red-headed, blue-eyed, two-year-old little boy. As to when this happened, I am mystified. Talk about a not-so-good-mommy-moment when my husband stood before me waiting for an explanation. It's not like I was back in my bedroom painting my nails while watching a movie (but doesn't that just sound so wonderful). I *was* watching the child, but somehow missed his whole undercover, 007 mission.

This memory makes me think about how we allow temptation into our lives. Jesus warns us to watch and pray because He knows it just takes a moment for us to be distracted. It just takes a few days away from His Word for our hearts to be hardened and lose our sensitive spirit towards His righteousness. It just takes a split-second decision to completely change our lives. It just takes experiencing or watching a few worldly situations to callous our thinking of what is right and wrong.

This is why it is so important to put on our full armor of God each day. We need to put on our belt of truth, the breastplate of righteousness, to have our feet fitted with the readiness that comes with peace, the shield of faith, the helmet of salvation and the sword of the Spirit. Not only do we need to be equipped, but we also need to be alert and *aware*. We need to be prepared for the traps the evil one likes to place, especially when we are most vulnerable. We cannot resist these alone, and God is calling us to ask Him for help. He wants to strengthen us for battle, He wants to equip us to stand strong, and He wants us to keep our eyes on Him so we are able to identify the temptations… and to keep a look out for those crazy hair dryers!

Heavenly Father, I come before You in need of your help. Help me to stand firm in Your truth. Keep my heart steadfast on You. Keep my mind fully on Your righteousness, Your spirit and Your Word. Give me the strength to stand my ground and resist all temptation that may come my way. In Jesus name, Amen.

—Natalie

Today God is stirring my heart by…

I WANT MORE!

"I know what it is to be in need, and I know what it is to have plenty. I have learned the secret of being content in any and every situation, whether well fed or hungry, whether living in plenty or in want."

Philippians 4:12

I want more! This is most likely an expression you are familiar with. We hear it daily and sometimes are the ones who demand more. I know I am guilty of that. When our youngest son Caleb was 15 months old, God got a hold of my heart and taught me an important lesson. It is a lesson I am still learning but I am so thankful God started a work in my heart that morning.

When Caleb was 15 months old, he was a hungry boy. He always wanted more. We taught our kids sign language before they could speak so we were able to communicate with them. Caleb would use the sign for 'more' very vigorously each day.

Almost every morning I fed Caleb his cereal. He was not quite ready to feed it to himself without making a big mess. Honestly, it was a little frustrating because my task oriented self wanted to be doing something else. But, God used that time to teach me.

The first lesson God has taught me is to focus on the here and now. This time feeding Caleb can be precious. I can choose to focus on loving him, serving him and meeting his needs. I am his Mom and that is what I am here for. Caleb depends on me to feed him and I can show him that I am trustworthy.

Caleb is a big eater and most of the time he can't seem to get enough. So, when I am feeding him, he will often grab at me for more even when he still has food in his mouth. This can be very annoying. But, again God taught me that I can be the same way with Him. He gives me my daily bread and yet I can be ungrateful and grab at Him for more. I don't necessarily need more since my mouth is already full. He wants me to be content with what I have. Wow, what a lesson! Paul knew the secret of being content. In Philippians 4:12, our key verse for today, we read "I know what it is to be in need, and I know what it is to have plenty. I have learned the secret of being content in any and every situation, whether well fed or hungry, whether living in plenty or in want." Contentment. So hard to do sometimes, but something I know I need to grow in.

The next time I go to feed Caleb his morning cereal, I know I will have a totally different perspective. I desire to be present with my kids. I don't want them to remember me as a Mom who accomplished lots of tasks around the house. I want to be remembered as a Mom who gave her full attention to her children when they spoke with her. I will also rejoice in the truth that God will provide all that I need. I choose to trust God to provide my daily bread. I also choose to be grateful for my daily bread.

God knows what I need. He knows what you need. Will you trust Him? Will you grab hold of Him and trust that He will give you what you need?

Heavenly Father, You are a good, good Father. Thank You for knowing every one of my needs and providing for each one. Please help me to be content with my daily bread. Help me to be a Mom who is focused on the here and now. I don't want to miss out on this very precious time with my kids. I love You, LORD. In Jesus name, Amen.

—Anastasia

Today God is stirring my heart by…

TAKE TIME
TO LISTEN

"Devote yourselves to prayer, being watchful and thankful."

Colossians 4:2

Last year I had a situation come up that left me feeling emotionally, physically and mentally exhausted. I found myself continually talking to the LORD about this situation that I continually mulled over in my mind. One day as I was talking to God about things, He gently reminded me that I was doing a lot of the talking. Ouch. We serve a mighty, compassionate, and caring God that loves when we go to Him and share what is on our hearts, but often time I find myself doing a lot of the talking in our relationship. I began to see that I'm never going to hear His voice if I keep talking over Him. I'm never going to see His direction if I don't pause long enough to hear Him say which way to go. How can I expect God to comfort me if I don't stop long enough for him to wrap His arms around my heart?

Have you noticed in the Bible when Jesus went to pray, many times he made a point to find a solitary place? In Mark 1:35 it says, "Very early in the morning, while it was still dark, Jesus got up, left the house and went off to a solitary place, where he prayed." And in Matthew 14:23 we see what Jesus did after a long day. "After he had dismissed the crowd, he went up on a mountainside by himself to pray." And the time when Jesus knew He needed to prepare His heart for what was next. "Then Jesus went with his disciples to a place called Gethsemane, and he said to them, 'Sit here while I go over there and pray.'" Matthew 26:36

I love when my days are full of talking with God, but it's been a good reminder to find those moments when my schedule and thoughts are busy to stop, pause, and listen *to what God wants to talk to me about!* You know what else hit me hard. Just being honest, but sometimes when I'm thinking about something or a situation, I constitute that as praying—when really it isn't.

Every morning when I take my kids to school, I pray over them. Well, when I was driving my kids to school I was "praying" (a.k.a— mulling over something in my head), and when we got right up to the school my son asked, "Mom, aren't you going to pray?" Let me tell you, there is nothing like being convicted *twice* before eight o'clock in the morning, and all in the time frame of about five seconds.

I became convicted of: #1—That I was so consumed with my thoughts that I missed an opportunity to pour into my kids. #2—I felt like through my son, God asked me, "Natalie, aren't you going to pray?" Instead of just thinking about it and mulling it over in my head while considering it praying, God wanted me to pause and *really* pray about it. How about you? Have you been thinking about something this week more than praying about it?

Heavenly Father, I come before You sharing my heart, but also wanting to hear Yours. Help me not to just talk to You, but to take the time to pause and listen. Gently remind me during the times that my thoughts are claiming too much time, to turn those thoughts over to You so instead of mulling it over, I'm handing it over! In Jesus name, Amen.

—Natalie

Today God is stirring my heart by…

A CHOICE
THAT CHANGES
EVERYTHING

"Then Jesus said, "Come to me, all of you who are weary and carry heavy burdens, and I will give you rest. Take my yoke upon you. Let me teach you, because I am humble and gentle at heart, and you will find rest for your souls. For my yoke is easy to bear, and the burden I give you is light."

Matthew 11:28–30, NLT

What if I told you that you were in control of what kind of day you would have? You have the power to decide if you're going to have a good day or a bad day.

I bet you're asking "What do you mean that I have a choice? What about that text I just received that shattered my world? What about that coworker that just slammed my character in front of everyone? How can I a good day with all this happening?" There are so many more questions that can be asked. How can we have a good day even in the middle of heartache and pain?

It's about a choice. A choice that changes everything. No matter what happens in our day, we have the power to choose what our attitude is going to be. Are we going to let the circumstances of life pull us down? Or will we choose to keep our eyes up on the only One that is constant in our life? Are we going to trust in ourselves or are we going to trust in God?

We are the only ones who can choose to have a good day. No one else can make this choice for us. How do we do this? How do we choose to have a good day? By turning to the God who holds the world in the palm of His hands. We need to give all that weighs heavy on our hearts to the One who sees everything and cares about every detail in our lives. When we place it all in God's hands and choose to focus on Him instead of our circumstances, we can have a good day. In fact, our day can be great!

This isn't easy to do. I know. It's still a struggle for me. It's hard to keep focused when the world around me is falling apart. But, I am going to keep making the choice that changes everything. Why? Because I know what it's like to feel deep heartache and yet also feel deep joy and peace. I know how much lighter I feel when I place my burdens in God's hands. And as I trust God more, I realize again and again how much He loves me and how much His plan is greater.

How about you? What kind of day will you have? It's your choice. A choice that changes everything.

Heavenly Father, I do have a choice each day. I want to make a choice that shows I completely trust in You. I want to remember all the ways You have come through before. I want to focus on You instead of my circumstances. Thank You that you never change and that I can count on You. Help me to make the choice that changes everything. I love you LORD. In Jesus name, Amen.

—Anastasia

Today God is stirring my heart by…

NOTHING
BUT THE TRUTH

"All Scripture is God-breathed and is useful for teaching, rebuking, correcting and training in righteousness, so that the man of God may be thoroughly equipped for every good work."

2 Timothy 3:16–17

My son Brayden loves to tell stories. It's so fun to watch his personality spring to life when he is telling a story and being the center of attention. I have no idea where he gets this from. I can't even write that with a straight face. However, when he was very little, sometimes I found myself wondering if what he was saying was true and what part of the story I could believe.

This made me think of how our society, and sadly, Christians have watered down God's Word. They take and use it when it applies to their life and ignore it when it doesn't suit them or their lifestyle. Some even claim that it is just a book of stories that don't have to be followed. In Jeremiah 36, King Jehoiakim was given a scroll from Jeremiah that held the Words of Lord on them. The King didn't like his message from the Lord, so he burnt the scroll. It seems a bit extreme, but how often do we do this on a lesser scale? We manipulate the scriptures to make ourselves feel better with how we are living our life and then excuse ourselves from living a righteous life, like we are told in the scriptures. We get ourselves in trouble when we don't believe the *whole and entire Bible as truth!*

If we can't trust scripture, we lose confidence in God. God's

Word, all of it, is living and active and it is the truth! It says in Hebrews 4:12, "For the word of God is living and active. Sharper than any double-edged sword, it penetrates even to dividing soul and spirit, joints and marrow; it judges the thoughts and attitudes of the heart." God gave us the Bible to direct us, show us how to live and act, as a tool to discern the truth, to encourage others, and it give us a glimpse of His heart. When we cut out a part of God's Word, we devalue Him. When God asked us to follow Him, He didn't ask for half, whatever we want to give or whenever it works for us. No, He asked for ALL. So why would God give us any less than that!

Heavenly Father, thank You for giving me Your Word that is true, life-changing and because it is God-breathed—it's full of new revelations daily. May I always hold Your Word as sacred and completely—cover to cover—full of truth. In Jesus name, Amen.

—Natalie

Today God is stirring my heart by...

HELP!

"Then they cried out to the Lᴏʀᴅ in their trouble, and he brought them out of their distress. He stilled the storm to a whisper; the waves of the sea were hushed. They were glad when it grew calm, and he guided them to their desired haven."

Psalm 107:28–30

Picture this familiar scene. It's quiet and calm on the home front. You're playing a game with one of your children and the other kids are downstairs playing together. And then you hear it. Screaming from one kid, yelling from the other and then "MOOOM, I need help!!!" Instead of staying where you are (which let's be honest, sometimes you want to), you head downstairs to see who the call for help came from. After investigating and hearing all sides of the story, you help the kids take care of the problem.

Does this ever happen in your home? I am sure it has on some occasion. As Moms, we are there to help our kids out of their troubles, even ones they have placed themselves in. It is in these times I have a greater appreciation of how God helps me. Our key verses for today have been ones of great comfort to me when I am dealing with a problem. It's packed with promises of how God takes care of us in the storms of life. God brings us out of our distress, stills the storm to a whisper, hushes the waves of the sea, and guides us to our desired haven.

God brings us out of our distress. What is distress? It is defined as trouble, pain, anxiety, or sorrow. In this Psalm, Israel's merchants are braving the sea to do some trading. They are in distress as the storm raged around them. They turned to God for help. The Israelites have learned that God can take care of them and bring them out of their distress. Do we have this same faith? Is God the first person we turn to in our distress? Do we trust His track record? God longs to bring us out of our distress. We just need to ask.

Not only does God bring us out of our distress, He also stills the storm to a whisper. There are times where the storms of life overwhelm us. It becomes too much to carry. It is in those moments that we need to let God handle the storm. Too often I try to push through a storm on my own strength. I become weary, discouraged and lose focus. Does this sound familiar to you? God can handle any storm in your life. We need to hand it back to God and let Him still it to a whisper.

Even when the storm is stilled, the waves of life can still be raging. We need to remember in that time who the Author of the sea is. God can hush the waves of the sea and because of that, things in life can be calm.

In this Psalm, the Israelite merchants were sailing to do some trading. After God calmed the storm, He guided them to the place they wanted to go. God also loves to guide us to our desired haven. He knows our needs before we even ask Him. But, God loves to hear from us. He loves it when we depend on Him instead of trying to get their on our own strength. Do you trust God to bring you to your desired haven?

God loves it when we cry to Him for help. He loves to respond in the way that we need in that moment. God always knows best and each situation is different. God is with us in the storms of life. He brings us out of our distress, stills the storm to a whisper, hushes the waves of the sea, and guides us to our desired haven. Will you cry out to God for help?

Heavenly Father, thank You that You are always available to help me. Thank You that no matter what storm I am facing in life You are there. Please help me to trust You to bring me out of my distress, still the storm, hush the waves, and guide me to my desired haven. In Jesus name, Amen.
—Anastasia

Today God is stirring my heart by…

THE
HOLY SPIRIT

"So I say, live by the Spirit, and you will not gratify the desires of the sinful nature. For the sinful nature desires what is contrary to the Spirit, and the Spirit what is contrary to the sinful nature. They are in conflict with each other, so that you do not do what you want. But if you are led by the Spirit, you are not under law."

Galatians 5: 16–18

The Father. The Son. The Holy Spirit. As I soak in the Trinity and what that means for believers, I can't help but wonder how much we are missing out in our spiritual walk when we lean heavier to God and Jesus, but discount the work of the Holy Spirit in our lives. It makes me think of when you take a picture using a tripod. If you aren't using each of the three legs equally, what happens to your picture? It's off center, crooked, not nearly as effective and you might miss the focus of your picture. Each leg is just as crucial as the other and they all have to work together on the same level to have the biggest impact.

God tells us in His Word how valuable and important His Holy Spirit is. The Holy Spirit speaks through us, He changes our hearts, helps us understand the Bible, convicts us, shows God's righteousness, guides and gives insight for the future, sets us free from sin and death, gives us the mind of Christ, and helps us pray.

Many times through scripture it even says that Jesus was filled with the Spirit. Jesus promised to pour out His Spirit on us in John

7:37–38, "On the last and greatest day of the Feast, Jesus stood and said in a loud voice, "If anyone is thirsty, let him come to me and drink. Whoever believes in me, as the Scripture has said, streams of living water will flow from within him." I don't know about you, but that makes me want to shout, "Fill me, LORD, fill me!" The presence of the Holy Spirit in our lives should demonstrate our genuineness of our faith, it proves that we are God's children, it transforms us, and it secures our eternal life.

We must not forget that God is very unyielding about the Holy Spirit in our lives. In Luke 12:10, Jesus says, "And everyone who speaks a word against the Son of Man will be forgiven, but anyone who blasphemes against the Holy Spirit will not be forgiven." And also in Ephesians 4:30, "And do not grieve the Holy Spirit of God, with whom you were sealed for the day of redemption." This happens when we have a deliberate and ongoing rejection of the Holy Spirit's work in our lives. It's when our hearts are so hardened that we shut ourselves off from God and don't acknowledge the sin in our lives.

The enemy's desire is to thwart God's kingdom and purposes, and an easy way to make that happen is to get believers to ignore the Holy Spirit. How does that apply to your life? Even though the Holy Spirit lives in us, we will still be tempted and sin, but we should be known by the fruit He produces in us. We can find those in Galatians 5:22–23, "But the fruit of the Spirit is love, joy, peace, patience, kindness, goodness, faithfulness, gentleness and self-control." So over the next few days we will be focusing on these fruits and how our lives can be full of them.

Heavenly Father, I welcome Your Holy Spirit into my life. Please guide my steps, speak my words, and convict my heart. Fill me LORD, fill me!!! Bring to light any sin that has grieved Your Spirit. Speak Your Truth into me and transform my life. In Jesus name, Amen.

—Natalie

Today God is stirring my heart by...

LOVE

"Love is patient, love is kind. It does not envy, it does not boast, it is not proud. It is not rude, it is not self-seeking, it is not easily angered, it keeps no record of wrongs. Love does not delight in evil but rejoices with the truth. It always protects, always trusts, always hopes, always perseveres. Love never fails."

1 Corinthians 13:4–8

I think the Bible is pretty clear on what the definition of love is. In 1 John 3:16 it also says, "This is how we know what love is: Jesus Christ laid down his life for us. And we ought to lay down our lives for our brothers." For fun, I asked my kids what they thought love meant. My two older boys both said that it was being kind to others and doing nice things for them. My five-year-old daughter said that love is when you ask someone their name and then tell them you love it (obviously we have a little work to do with this child… but really, cutest response ever!)

God is love. In fact, the great commandment that the LORD gives us is in Matthew 22:37–38, "Love the LORD your God with all your heart and with all your soul and with all your mind. This is the first and greatest commandment. And the second is like it: Love your neighbor as yourself." Love can come so easy, until it's not. I think the hardest time in marriage, parenting, friendships, and relationships, is having to love someone when you don't feel like it. Love is the most amazing feeling, and yet, true love isn't the emotion, it's the choice.

We have to choose to love and follow God when the desire and feelings aren't there. We have to choose to love others even if there isn't an ounce of desire or feelings to do so. Not only is God very passionate about loving us, and because of that love we in turn love Him and others, but He is very stern about harboring hatred in our hearts. It says in, 1 John 4:19–21 "We love because he first loved us. If anyone says, "I love God," yet hates his brother, he is a liar. For anyone who does not love his brother, whom he has seen cannot love God, whom he has not seen. And he has given us this command: Whoever loves God must also love his brother."

It's easy to love others when it doesn't cost us anything. The real test—the fruit we produce from the Holy Spirit—is how we treat others right in front of us. Today, bask in the truth that God wants to lavish His love on you. He loves you so incredibly much. Let Him fill you of that love so that it may overflow onto others around you!

Heavenly Father, thank You for loving me and calling me Your child. Let me not only love with words or tongue, but with actions and in truth. For this is love: not that I loved You, but that You loved me and sent your Son as an atoning sacrifice for my sins. Because You love me, help me to love others. No one has ever seen you God, but if I love others, You will live in me and Your love is made complete in me!" In Jesus name, Amen.

—Natalie

Today God is stirring my heart by…

JOY

"Be joyful always."

1 Thessalonians 5:16

There is a fine line between joy and happiness. Happiness is the state of being happy. It's when the circumstances around you stir the emotions that bring pleasure, delight, well-being and enjoyment. Joy is knowing that God has control over every detail of your life and you make the choice to praise God in every situation. Joy doesn't come from our surroundings, but it's birthed in our hearts and souls.

My mother-in-law was a great testimony to me about this very thing. I only knew her for a year, but her impression will last a lifetime. She dealt with cancer for years, the kind that makes you wonder how a human can possibly handle something so painful and horrible, and I never, ever saw her lose her joy. Even on her death bed she had a smile on her face through the tears, praising God.

When we truly walk in the Spirit of joy, it is our core foundation. We will still have sadness, heartache, pain, mourning… but we will have the ability to know that God is good, faithful and that there is so much more beyond the moment. It says in Proverbs 31:25, "She is clothed with strength and dignity; she can laugh at the days to come." We are strong when our focus is on God, not on our situations. We have the ability to laugh at the days to come when we know that God is in control of them.

God tells us in Nehemiah 8:10 "The joy of the LORD is our strength." So if joy is our strength, then obviously Satan wants to take that from us. The thief comes only to steal and kill and destroy; but Jesus came that we may have life, and have it to the full. When we are strong, we are a threat to Satan and his work, but if we are weak, it gives the enemy a great opportunity to suffocate us, press us under his thumb, and take advantage of our weakness. It is God's will for us to enjoy life and live it full of joy. Today we have a choice to make the decision to walk a life of joy and praise him for who He is—to stand firmly in Isaiah 12:2–3, "Surely God is my salvation; I will trust and not be afraid. The LORD, the LORD, is my strength and my song; he has become my salvation. With joy you will draw water from the wells of salvation."

Heavenly Father, rise up in me a strength that will not waver in times of trials. Give me a cheerful heart that refreshes my soul and fills me with a joy that can only come from You. In Jesus name, Amen.

—Natalie

Today God is stirring my heart by…

PEACE

"Jesus replied, 'If anyone loves me, he will obey my teaching. My Father will love him, and we will come to him and make our home with him. He who does not love me will not obey my teaching. These words you hear are not my own; they belong to the Father who sent me. All this I have spoken while still with you. But the Counselor, the Holy Spirit, whom the Father will send in my name, will teach you all things and will remind you of everything I have said to you. Peace I leave you; my peace I give you. I do not give to you as the world gives. Do not let your hearts be troubled and do not be afraid.'"

John 14: 23–27

When Jesus left us physically, He left us with the gift of peace through His Holy Spirit. Peace is a tool to use in our journey of life as we follow after Him—A way to hear direction and to know if we are walking in His path. Peace is to be our guide. When we don't feel peace, that should be an indicator that something isn't right. That we are to pause and spend time searching God's heart so we are better able to hear the direction He is nudging us to go. If we don't have peace, we need to dig deep and figure out why.

Even though peace is a gift, it takes an effort on our part to receive it. In Psalm 34:14 it says, "Turn from evil and do good, seek peace and pursue it." Many times we don't feel peace because we aren't walking in the LORD's will. Not very often in the Bible will you find the word peace without the word righteousness near it. In Psalm

85:10 it says, "Love and faithfulness meet together; righteousness and peace kiss each other." I love this verse. You can't get much closer than two lips smooched together!

Often times we have situations arise in our lives that bring worry upon us that strangles our peace or we have huge decisions to make and it's hard to know what we are called to do. In Philippians 4:6–7 it says, "Do not be anxious about anything, but in everything, by prayer and petition, with thanksgiving, present your requests to God. And the peace of God, which transcends all understanding, will guard your hearts and your minds in Christ Jesus."

I don't know about you, but my peace is taken from me when I sin and I need to ask for forgiveness. When I know I should do something, but don't. When my mouth runs because my emotions have taken control. Are you struggling with peace in a certain area in your life? I encourage you to step back, figure out why, ask God for peace, and then pursue Him whole-heartily until you receive it!

Heavenly Father, thank You for your gift of peace. You have said in your word that You are not a God of disorder, but of peace. Help me claim Your peace over my life today. I want to live a righteous life for You— show me the best ways to pursue You. In Jesus name, Amen.

—Natalie

Today God is stirring my heart by...

PATIENCE

"Be completely humble and gentle; be patient, bearing with one another in love."

Ephesians 4:2

Patience. In the world of motherhood, don't we speak this word many times to the LORD, asking Him to give us patience toward our kids, husband, or anyone that dares to cross our path after a sleepless night? When looking at the fruits of the Spirit, I'd say this one is a big struggle for me. Especially in the morning when I'm rushing around trying to get three kids ready, fed, lunches made, and everyone out the door for school. I'll admit, once we all get in the van, about twice a week I have to ask God and my kids for forgiveness because my patience has unraveled. It's the constant repeating, constant reminding, constant finding lost items because they weren't put where they belong in the first place, and constant pulling kids out of bed that can really grate on my nerves. Some days I'd rather go to the dentist, get my blood drawn, or have a full gynecologist exam than deal with it. However, this is the season I am in, so I need to make the most of it.

So why does God tell us we need to be patient? Well, I don't know about you, but when I'm not patient I usually don't possess any of the other fruits of the Spirit. When I lose my patience it reminds me of Proverbs 14:29, "A patient man has great understanding, but a quick-tempered man displays his folly." And sadly a lot more folly is going on than understanding. God tells us that love is patient. And who is God? God is love. So when we are not patient, we are not being Christ-like.

God is so incredibly patient with us as we walk along, fumbling and rushing around in this life. He is constantly and consistently repeating and reminding us, and yet He responds with patience every single time even though we struggle with the same thing over and over again. He is patient as we learn, as we make mistakes, and as we unfold the wonders of who He is.

As mothers we are to raise our children to be disciples. I read a verse that gently convicted me about the impact that I make on my children. 2 Timothy 4:1–2, "In the presence of God and of Christ Jesus, who will judge the living and the dead, and in view of his appearing and his kingdom. I give you this charge: Preach the Word; be prepared in season and out of season; correct, rebuke and encourage—with great patience and careful instruction." Paul charges us to preach the word and be ready to serve the LORD in any situation or season.

How do we do that? By great patience—and we can get this by seeking God and focusing on Him, not our situations. We also need to identify what causes us to lose our patience, so maybe ask the questions: Why are you in a hurry? Can you recognize the triggers that cause impatience? Can you see the patterns? What can you change?

Paul tells us that we also need to be prepared to serve God with careful instruction. This is a huge responsibility and in order to instruct our children, we must be saturated in the Word so that when the time comes we are speaking truth and we are careful with our response.

Heavenly Father, thank You for showing me the perfect example of patience. Help me to clothe myself with compassion, kindness, humility, gentleness and patience and over all these virtues to put on love, which binds them all together. Guide me as I lead my children and show me ways to be an example of how to have great patience and careful instruction. In Jesus name, Amen.

—Natalie

Today God is stirring my heart by…

KINDNESS

"For this very reason, make every effort to add to your faith goodness; and to goodness, knowledge; and to knowledge, self-control; and to self-control, perseverance; and to perseverance, godliness; and to godliness, brotherly kindness; and to brotherly kindness, love. For if you possess these qualities in increasing measure, they will keep you from being ineffective and unproductive in your knowledge of our Lord Jesus Christ. But if anyone does not have them, he is nearsighted and blind, and has forgotten that he has been cleansed from his past sins."

2 Peter 1:5–9

Kindness is the quality of being friendly, generous, and considerate. Kindness in definition is a noun, but to me, it's a verb. Kindness is performing a kind, considerate or helpful act. Kindness is an expression of words with intentions to create good around them and to warm the hearts of others. When I think of kindness, it can be the most heart-stirring when it is unexpected and selfless.

There is a person in the Bible that sticks out to me who defines kindness by the way he lived his life with his words and actions. Boaz. I think the book of Ruth is one of my favorites in the Bible. Ruth is such an inspiration to me. I'm humbled by the way Boaz lived his life. And let's be honest, it's a beautiful love story.

Boaz enters the scene as Ruth is out gleaning in his fields. Boaz arrives and he greets his harvesters with kindness, "The Lord be with you!" Boaz was a wealthy man of great importance and treated everyone around him with sincere respect. He then asks his foreman who the woman in the field was and became informed of all Ruth's history. Boaz then goes to Ruth and tells her not to glean in another field, to stay with his servant girls, told his men not to touch her, and that whenever she was thirsty to get a drink from the water jars… and then he praises her with kind words for all she had done for her mother in law, Naomi. After, he had her join him at meal time and then privately told his workers to let some of the grain fall in her path. Later on, Ruth approaches him and asks him to become her kinsman-redeemer. He agrees, gives her more barley, and then handles the situation right away with integrity. What a perfect example of kindness in action.

God tells us to be filled with the Spirit—and a fruit of His Spirit is kindness. Let's look a bit deeper into the Word about kindness. It says in Proverbs 14:21, "He who despises his neighbor sins, but blessed is he who is kind to the needy." God will bless us by our kindness. The word needy sticks out to me in this verse. Needy often means poor (and we of course need to be kind to the poor), but let's take a step further. To me, needy means that someone is lacking something—whether it's money, companionship, confidence, encouragement, hope, etc. There are so many ways God has called us to kindness.

God says in Ephesians 5:15–16, "Be very careful, then, how you live—not as unwise but as wise, making the most of every opportunity, because the days are evil." Make the most of your day today. Be proactive in ways you can be kind to the "needy." Look for opportunities to make kindness into a verb.

Heavenly Father, You are the creator of kindness, there is no better example to find. You are perfect in every way and Your kindness is everlasting. Show me today how I can step out and live a life saturated in kindness. And that whatever I do, whether in word or deed, may I do it all in the name of the LORD Jesus, giving thanks to God. In Jesus name, Amen.

—Natalie

Today God is stirring my heart by…

GOODNESS

"You are good, and what you do is good; teach me your decrees."

Psalm 119:68

When you line up all the fruits of the Spirit, I find that goodness is at the foundation of them. In our humanness, the only time we do something good is because of God. God is good. Everything He does is good. So when we allow Him to fill us, that is the ONLY reason we can produce good fruit. The only thing good in us is God. When we are filled with God's goodness, isn't it so much easier to express love, joy, peace, patience, kindness, faithfulness, gentleness, and self-control.

In Matthew 7:16–20, Jesus speaks about how we will be recognized by our fruit. "By their fruit you will recognize them. Do people pick grapes from thorn bushes, or figs from thistles? Likewise every good tree bears good fruit, but a bad tree bears bad fruit. A good tree cannot bear bad fruit, and a bad tree cannot bear good fruit. Every tree that does not bear good fruit is cut down and thrown into the fire. Thus, by their fruit you will recognize them."

Each day I need to desire and pursue a life that bears fruit that others will recognize me as not only a Christ follower, but someone that is filled with goodness, because what I am filled with will overflow from within me. What I harbor in my heart will determine my words, my thoughts, and my actions. Jesus once again talks about this in Matthew 12:33–35, "Make a tree good and its fruit will be good, or make a tree bad and its fruit will be bad, for a tree is recognized by its fruit. You brood of vipers, how can you who are evil say anything good? For out of the overflow of the heart the mouth speaks. The good man brings good things out of the good stored up in him, and the evil man brings things out of the evil stored up in him."

Each day, every moment, I need to work at storing up good within me by spending time in the Word and soaking up its truths, by praying and deepening my relationship with God, and by pausing and listening to how He wants to fill me with His goodness.

Heavenly Father, there is only One who is good, and that is You. You are virtuous, excellent and upright. LORD, open my eyes and turn me from darkness to light so that if there is any corner within me that harbors evil, that I may turn it to good. Help me to be a good tree that bears good fruit. In Jesus name, Amen.

—Natalie

Today God is stirring my heart by…

FAITHFULNESS

"Your kingdom is an everlasting kingdom, and your dominion endures through all generations. The LORD is faithful to all his promises and loving toward all he has made."

Psalm 145:13

There are many ways you can be reassured in God, and faithfulness is one of them. God has promised that He is worthy of our trust, devotion and loyalty. Now we just have to believe it. When we are filled with the Spirit, then our faithfulness in the one true God should overflow out of us and into our words and actions.

When I think of faithfulness, I always think of the parable Jesus shared about the talents in Matthew 25:14–30. "Again, it will be like a man going on a journey, who called his servants and entrusted his property to them. To one he gave five talents of money, to another two talents, and to another one talent, each according to his ability. Then he went on his journey. The man who had received the five talents went at once and put his money to work and gained five more. So also, the one with the two talents gained two more. But the man who had received the one talent went off, dug a hole in the ground, and hid his master's money."

The parable continues that the man came back to see how his servants did with their talents. He applauded the men that had doubled their talents by saying, "Well done, good and faithful servant! You have been faithful with a few things; I will put you in charge of many things. Come and share your master's happiness!" But for the last servant that buried his talents, the man called him a wicked and lazy servant and threw him outside. I don't know about you, but my heart's desire is to be faithful in whatever God gives me.

I felt the LORD tell me once when I was sharing with Him about my huge hopes and dreams, that if I wasn't faithful to God in the small things, how can He expect me to be faithful in the big things! Every step we take, every situation we are in, is a time of preparation for what God has in store for us next. Life is a process and He is always in the midst of working in your life. However, please hear me, if you are living a lifestyle that does not line up with God's Word or His truth—that is NOT where He has called you.

When I think about the talents, I understand as believers how we can get frustrated. We look around and think that we don't measure up. Our purpose doesn't feel as important as those around us. I often wonder what the man with one talent was thinking. He seemed scared of what to do with his talent. Did he think, "I only have one talent, it's not a big deal, what does it matter if I just sit on it?" Let me tell you, it DOES matter. We are responsible to use what God has given us. We shouldn't be concerned about what He has given us compared to others, but how well we use what we have.

So today I want to encourage you to be faithful in where God has you right now and the talents He has given you. If you want God to expand your territory, be faithful in the reach He has given you now. If you want Him to entrust you with more money, be faithful in what He has given you now. If you want to step out in a new role (whether with ministry or a job), then be faithful in the place he has called you now. If you want to be filled with wisdom, then be faithful in asking for it, digging into the Word and applying it to your life. Take a moment to pause and ask God to show you ways in how you can be better faithful to Him right where you are.

Heavenly Father, You are the perfect example of faithfulness. For You, O LORD, love the just and will not forsake his faithful ones (Psalm 37:28). Fill me with Your Spirit so that I may be in tune with Your will and ways. Grant me the ability to take the talents that You have given me and use them to further Your kingdom. In Jesus name, Amen.

—Natalie

Today God is stirring my heart by…

GENTLENESS

*"Your beauty should not come from outward adornment,
such as braided hair and the wearing of gold jewelry and
fine clothes. Instead, it should be that of your inner self, the
unfading beauty of a gentle and quiet spirit, which is of
great worth in God's sight."*

1 Peter 3:3–4

Gentleness. I'll be honest with you for a moment. I have to work really hard at this fruit. It's not a natural response for me, especially as a mother. I came across a verse that squeezed my heart. 1 Thessalonians 2:6–7, "We were not looking for praise from men, not from you or anyone else. As apostles of Christ we could have been a burden to you, but we were gentle among you, like a mother caring for her little children." Whoops. I hear you, LORD.

A few years ago I started having a "theme" word that I wanted to work on for the year, and the last two years it has been the same word: Gentleness. Have you stopped lately and considered how gentle God is with you? As I sit here and think about that I'm overwhelmed by the many times He has corrected me by His still small voice, without condemnation, but by a stirring of conviction as He refocuses my heart and thoughts with gentleness. And even when it's the one hundredth time He had to do it that day, He is so patient and gentle with me. Then I think of my kids and how I lose my cool after they ask for gum, candy, electronics, or say my name for the umpteenth time, and then I realize I still have much more work to do. It might be my word for next year as well.

Throughout the Gospels we have a great example of gentleness by watching Jesus walk on earth and interact with people. Many people would cling on to Him asking for healing, and He responded with gentleness. All day He would be bombarded with questions, some asking about the Kingdom, some trying to make Him stumble, some persecuting for what He stood for, and each time He responded with gentleness. Even when the guards came to arrest Him, He handled the situation with gentleness. When it comes to gentleness, I don't think God's intention is to have people walk all over us or take advantage of us. We can still be firm, assertive, and not timid—but wrapped in gentleness. Gentleness is love in action. It's a response. It's an attitude. It's respecting and being considerate to others. An example of this is from Proverbs 15:1 "A gentle answer turns away wrath, but a harsh word stirs up anger."

One day I took my kids out for dinner while my husband was out of town. It was a sit down restaurant, so I knew it would take longer, but I hadn't expected the extreme delay in service. It took our waitress almost fifteen minutes to return with our drinks and to take our food order. Needless to say, I was upset. With each passing minute my plan burned from frustration and I was ready to get a manager and let them know how I felt about the service. Then my son did something I will never forget. He asked me for a napkin because he wanted to write the waitress a letter. It said, "Thank you for your kindness. Love, Brayden." He gave it to her and she smiled at him, thanking him over and over for how sweet he was. When she left he had tears in his eyes, so I asked him if he was okay. He said, "Yes, I just like making other people happy!" By his simple act, he made that girl's night, while I stewed on how to prove a point. Not my finest moment. I wish I could say this was the only time where my children humbled me by handling a situation better than me. When God said we would be known by our fruit, one way it means is that we would be known by our gentleness. Philippians 4:5 says, "Let your gentleness be evident to all. The LORD is near." Are there ways in your life that you could use an extra dose of gentleness?

Heavenly Father, I ask that You would reveal to me the areas where I need to display more gentleness. Before I react, help me to pause and realize how I can respond with gentleness so that I can improve the situation and to be a better example to lead others to You. In Jesus name, Amen.

—Natalie

Today God is stirring my heart by…

SELF-CONTROL

"For this reason, make every effort to add to your faith goodness; and to goodness, knowledge; and to knowledge, self-control; and to self-control, perseverance; and to perseverance, godliness; and to godliness, brotherly kindness; and to brotherly kindness, love. For if you possess these qualities in increasing measure, they will keep you from being ineffective and unproductive in your knowledge of our LORD Jesus Christ. But if anyone does not have them, he is nearsighted and blind, and has forgotten that he has been cleansed from his past sins."

2 Peter 1:5–9

Self-Control is our last fruit of the spirit… and one that puts it all together. Self-Control is doing what you should do, not what you want to do. Self-Control is responding instead of reacting. Self-Control is dying to our flesh over and over and over again. The Bible tells us in Proverbs 23:28, "Like a city whose walls are broken down is a man who lacks self-control." Back then, they had walls up protecting their cities from marauders passing by. If their walls were broken down, they were vulnerable to the enemy. And that is what God is telling us. If we lack self-control, we lose a defense strategy against Satan. In turn, we are more susceptible to losing control when a situation arises and it will be easier to fall into the trap of sin.

That is why God encourages us to put on our armor each day. 1 Thessalonians 5:4–8 says, "But you are not in darkness so that this day should surprise you like a thief. You are all sons of the light and sons of the day. We do not belong to the night or to the darkness. So then, let us not be like others, who are asleep, but let us be alert and self-controlled. For those who sleep, sleep at night, and those who get drunk, get drunk at night. But since we belong to the day, let us be self-controlled, putting on faith and love as a breastplate, and the hope of salvation as a helmet."

Another way to look at what self-control means for us is to live a life that is disciplined. God tells us in 1 Peter 1:13–15, "Therefore, prepare your minds for action; be self-controlled; set your hope fully on the grace to be given you when Jesus Christ is revealed. As obedient children, do not conform to the evil desires you had when you lived in ignorance. But just as he who called you is holy, so be holy in all you do; for it is written; "Be holy, because I am holy."

God has set the bar impossibly high so that we understand how much we need Him. I love that part of scripture that says prepare your minds for action. That is why God tells us to consistently be in the Word and to pray without ceasing so that we can build our city walls high and strong. We are in the midst of the greatest and most strategic battle of our lives. Don't fight unprepared and unprotected. Are there any broken walls in your life that need rebuilt?

Heavenly Father, only You can help me to say "no" to ungodliness and worldly passions, and to live a self-controlled, upright, and godly life (Titus 2:12). Show me the areas in my life where my walls are broken and help me to build them one block at a time with love, joy, peace, patience, kindness, goodness, faithfulness, gentleness and self-control. In Jesus name, Amen.

—Natalie

Today God is stirring my heart by…

THE MOST IMPORTANT INGREDIENT

"Then Jesus declared, "I am the bread of life. Whoever comes to me will never go hungry, and whoever believes in me will never be thirsty."

John 6:35

Monday morning is my time to make homemade bread. Last week when I made it, I forgot the most important ingredient—yeast. You can imagine how flat my bread was. The funny thing is that I was so excited because I put the bread in before getting the kids off to school so I felt super accomplished. I LOVE to accomplish tasks. In fact, a good day for me is when I have crossed of lots of things off my 'to-do' list. In forgetting the yeast, God opened my eyes and taught me a few things. Who would have thought a jar of yeast could teach so much? I love how my God speaks through the most ordinary things. He used a jar of yeast to remind me of two things. Number one: what the most important ingredient of my day is and two: the truth about what defines a good day.

What is my yeast for my day? What is the one thing I need to have energy to keep going, so I am not flat by the end of the day? The most important ingredient in my day is time with Jesus. Time with only Him, my Bible, journal, and a pen. I absolutely love this time! Time to dig deep into His truth and feed on the true bread of life.

I didn't always have this deep longing to be with Him. In fact, it was something I wanted but didn't know how to attain. I remember my friend encouraging me to just spend time daily in the word and pray for a hunger for it. So, I did. Day by day I would take time even when I didn't feel like it, or when I didn't hear anything or when I only had a few minutes. Just as it takes time for bread to rise and then bake, it takes time for your relationship with Jesus to grow. You can't get to know a person well without spending time with them. It is the same with Jesus.

Another way Jesus spoke to me with forgetting the yeast was to look at how I define a good day. As I mentioned earlier a good day is accomplishing tasks for me. This is important and part of who I am. But, the real truth is a good day is when I take time to be with my Jesus. When I take time to listen to His voice, read His love letter, worship Him. When I do this, I know my friends and family are appreciative. I am more patient, kind, loving and others focused because of it.

What is the most important ingredient of your day? I want to encourage you to take time for the most important ingredient—Jesus. Take time daily to be in His word. Take time to listen to His voice.

Heavenly Father, You are the most ingredient of my day. Just like bread needs yeast to rise, I need You to rise above whatever comes my way. Please help me to remember to make the time to be with You each day. I want to dig deep into Your word and know Your heart more. In Jesus name, Amen.

—Anastasia

Today God is stirring my heart by…

WHAT DO YOU WANT ME TO DO FOR YOU?

"Jesus stopped and called them. "What do you want me to do for you?" he asked. "LORD," they answered, "we want our sight." Jesus had compassion on them and touched their eyes. Immediately they received their sight and followed him."

Matthew 20:32–34

When is the last time you really, really wanted something? I mean REALLY wanted something. You spent time dreaming about where it would go in your home or how great you would look in that new outfit. Or maybe you spent time imagining what it would be like to finally have someone in your life. Whatever it may be, we have all really wanted something in our life.

Here's a story from Matthew 20:29–31 about two men who really wanted something.

"As Jesus and his disciples were leaving Jericho, a large crowd followed him. Two blind men were sitting by the roadside, and when they heard that Jesus was going by, they shouted, "LORD, Son of David, have mercy on us!" The crowd rebuked them and told them to be quiet, but they shouted all the louder, "LORD, Son of David, have mercy on us!"

As I read this account, I was challenged to look at where I go when I really want something. These two men taught me a few things.

First, don't stop asking. These men sat by the roadside and heard Jesus was going by. Can you imagine how fast their hearts were beating? They had heard about this man named Jesus and they knew He could help them. So, they shouted out to Jesus. People all around them told them to be quiet. But instead of letting that stop them, they shouted all the louder. They got Jesus' attention.

Second, surround yourself with people who will encourage you to depend on God. The crowd rebuked these men for shouting at Jesus. What they needed in that moment was a friend to stop Jesus and point them out. They needed friends who were willing to do anything to help them get to Jesus. Do you have friends like that? We need to surround ourselves with people who point us to Jesus.

And finally, these men taught me to ask Jesus first and trust that He will provide. In Matthew 20:32–24, we see how bold these men were—"Jesus stopped and called them. "What do you want me to do for you?" he asked. "Lord," they answered, "we want our sight." Jesus had compassion on them and touched their eyes. Immediately they received their sight and followed him."

Too often I find myself asking others for help first instead of depending on the only One who can provide for all my needs. These men were very bold to yell out to Jesus. They did it because they knew He could heal them. I want that kind of faith, don't you? I love how Jesus blessed them because they chose to trust Him.

Jesus is asking you today "What do you want me to do for you?" Will you respond with what is on your heart? And then will you choose to trust Him?

Heavenly Father, I want to be like these men. I want to turn to You first. Please help me to do that. Thank You that You care so deeply for every one of my needs. Thank You that You want to provide. Please teach me to trust You more. In Jesus name, Amen.

—Anastasia

Today God is stirring my heart by…

MY CHRISTMAS MESS

"This is the day the Lord has made. We will rejoice and be glad in it."

Psalm 118:34, NLT

What a mess! There is about seven or eight loads of laundry that need to be folded. The very full baskets are behind a door but they still mocks me and tell me I am failure. The kitchen sink is full of dishes and we are about to make more of a mess with our breakfast. The house is overall messy and I have not kept up with things like I have wanted to. Our traditions have not been the same this year. I am sad and disappointed because things have not gone the way I've wanted.

This gives you a picture of what Christmas morning started off like for me this year. I was in a pouty mood and honestly felt so tired and worn out. I asked God to change my heart and speak to me in a powerful way. I didn't want to feel like this all day. This was Christmas after all. I didn't want to miss celebrating Jesus' birthday.

As we were making breakfast, I opened the egg carton and found our key verse from Psalm 118:34, "This is the day the Lord has made. We will rejoice and be glad in it." In that moment, I felt so loved and cared for. God cared enough about me to place that egg carton in the right place at the right time. He knew my heart needed to hear that truth. God created this day as a gift. No matter what mess and chaos surrounded me, I could choose to rejoice and be glad in it. The key in this was that I had to make a choice. A choice to rejoice.

As we continued preparing Christmas breakfast, my husband and I talked about how to Jesus came to earth as a baby into a very messy stable. Jesus chose to set aside the good things of heaven to come down to a place of disappointment and mess. Jesus knew what a mess He was coming into but chose to come anyway. Why? Because God loved us so much and wanted to spend eternity with us. Jesus came into the world to die so that we may have life. Jesus knew how his life on earth was going to end, yet He choose to come anyway.

Aren't you so glad Jesus came? I am. As I looked around at all the mess, I whispered a prayer of thanks to God for sending His One and Only son to the messy stable that Christmas morning. I also thanked Him for refocusing my heart on where it needed to be. I made a commitment to rejoice in the day that God had made.

How about you? Will you choose to rejoice in the day the LORD has made? Will you choose to look past the mess and disappointments and focus on the gift today is?

Heavenly Father, thank You for gift of a new day. Thank You for coming as a baby so long ago into this messy and disappointing world so that I may have eternal life. Please help me to rejoice in this day no matter how messy the house is or what disappointments I may face today. Thank You for loving me. In Jesus name, Amen.

—Anastasia

Today God is stirring my heart by…

LOOK UP

"Lift up your eyes and look to the heavens: Who created all these? He who brings out the starry host one by one and calls forth each of them by name. Because of his great power and mighty strength, not one of them is missing."

Isaiah 40:26

The other morning I went on a run. All too often I get caught up, meeting up with a friend for a run. But this particular morning, I stood in awe of God's creation. The stars were absolutely breathtaking. There were too many for me to count. As I stood there taking it all in, I couldn't help but be reminded that God created every single one of those stars. Every. Single. One. And not only did God create them, He brought the starry host out one by one. He called them forth by name. Did you catch that? By name. I love how detailed God is.

In that moment, I was reminded that if God can do that and hold the entire universe in balance, then He can definitely take care of me. I believe that when we look up, God shows us how he has called us, He reminds us whose we are and that He cares about every detail of our lives.

God called the starry host out one by one. God has called you too. If you are God's child, the calling on your life is very clear. In Matthew 29:18–20, we read "Then Jesus came to them and said, "All authority in heaven and on earth has been given to me. Therefore go and make disciples of all nations, baptizing them in the name of the Father and of the Son and of the Holy Spirit, and teaching them to obey everything I have commanded you. And surely I am with you always, to the very end of the age." Before Jesus left earth,

He made sure His disciples knew their mission in life. Our mission is the same. God has called us to live our lives for His glory and tell others about Him.

When we look up, God also reminds us whose we are. In Psalm 139:14, we read "I praise you because I am fearfully and wonderfully made; your works are wonderful, I know that full well." You are God's child, and because of that the truth is you are valuable. In Galatians 4:7 we read "So you are no longer a slave, but God's child; and since you are his child, God has made you also an heir." You are a daughter of the King of Kings and Creator of the whole universe. That makes you an heir. You are special. There are days you may not feel this way, but if God says it, it's true.

The other thing we remember when we look up is that God cares about every detail of our lives. In our key verse for today, we read "He who brings out the starry host one by one and calls forth each of them by name." God called every star by name. There are billions and billions of stars in our universe and God gave them each a name. God is a God of details. He cares about the details of your life even more. There is nothing about your life God doesn't already know. There is nothing that will happen today that God is not aware of. He is in control.

Will you choose to look up today? Will you choose to put your focus on the One who has called you by name? Will you walk with your head held high because you are a daughter of the King of Kings? Will you trust God with the details of your life? These questions convict me too. Let's walk this out together.

Heavenly Father, I want to look up and put my focus where it belongs. Please help me to walk with my head held high. Please help me to take You at Your word and believe I am incredibly valuable to You. God, I choose to trust You with the details of my life. Thank You for caring about every single one. I love You, LORD. In Jesus name, Amen.

—Anastasia

Today God is stirring my heart by...

I JUST CLEANED THE KITCHEN

"Whatever you do, work at it with all your heart, as working for the LORD, not for humans."

Colossians 3:23

Are you one of those people that love a clean kitchen? Does it energize and empower you? Me too. When my house is out of order, I feel like I am out of order. The other day my kitchen counters were cluttered with papers that needing to be filed, thrown away, and mail that still needed to be read. The pile of dirty dishes had grown out of the sink and invaded the remaining counter space. The dried on food mocked me from between the plates. Once again it was out of control… I felt defeated even before I had begun to fight back. Sometimes I wonder why I even bother to clean. It's only going to get messy again. Oh well, here I go. It has to be done. I rolled up my sleeves and whipped that kitchen into shape. The counters sparkled from the wash down, the dishwasher hummed quietly and no papers cluttered my counters. I could picture myself wearing the first place blue ribbon.

My accomplishment was soon dashed when not even a half an hour later the counters had been overtaken and the sink was overflowing with dirty dishes. Seriously?? I JUST cleaned the kitchen! Who made this mess? Will this ever stay clean? Which one of my kids did this? You could see smoke coming out of my ears from a mile away.

It was in that moment that God whispered to my heart. He asked me, "What are you focusing on right now? The fact that your kitchen isn't clean or the reason your kitchen isn't clean?" In that moment, I realized my focus was on the appearance of my kitchen. I like a clean kitchen and there is nothing wrong with that. I needed to choose in that moment to focus on why the kitchen was messy yet again. There was a mess because my family enjoyed a meal and had their needs met. We had enjoyed time around the table together and memories were made. In that moment, my perspective changed on a messy kitchen.

Now, instead of being irritated when my kitchen is messy, I am going to rejoice in the fact that we spent time together as a family. I will choose to look at cleaning the kitchen as a way of serving my family and providing a place for us all to grow.

I'm so thankful God spoke to my heart that day. I have so much more joy when I clean up the kitchen for the third or fourth time in a day. Yes, I still love a clean kitchen and I always will. But, now I am focusing on serving God instead of achieving my own success.

Heavenly Father, thank You for the gift of a messy kitchen. Please help me to focus more on the reason it is a mess instead of the mess itself. God, You have blessed me with a wonderful family. I want to focus on making memories with them and meeting their needs. Thank You for the gift of my family. Thank You for changing my focus. I love You, LORD. In Jesus name, Amen.

—Anastasia

Today God is stirring my heart by...

IMMEDIATELY

"But Jesus immediately said to them: "Take courage! It is I. Don't be afraid."

Matthew 14:27

As I read in Matthew 14 today, I was struck by the word immediately. So, I looked it up in the dictionary. I was blessed as I read the definition. The definition of immediately is: without lapse of time, without delay, instantly, at once. My God is an immediately God.

The disciples were in a boat being pushed around by the wind. When they saw Jesus walking on water they were afraid. In Matthew 14:27, we read "But Jesus IMMEDIATELY said to them: "Take courage! It is I. Don't be afraid." I love how Jesus responded to the fears of the disciples. He does the same for us. He asks us to trust Him. Like Peter, we wonder and question about the next step in life or even the next step in a day. I love how Jesus takes care of Peter as he steps out in faith.

"'Lord, if it's you,' Peter replied, 'tell me to come to you on the water.' 'Come,' he said. Then Peter got down out of the boat, walked on the water and came toward Jesus. But when he saw the wind, he was afraid and, beginning to sink, cried out, 'Lord, save me!'" (Matthew 14:28-30).

We can learn a lot from Peter in this account. First, we need to trust that God will take care of us when we take a step of faith. Did you notice where Peter had his eyes when he walked on the water? Peter had his eyes on Jesus. Why did Peter start to sink? He looked at the wind instead of Jesus. Like Peter, we also need to keep our eyes on Jesus instead of the storm brewing around us. We also learn that

Jesus is the One who can save us. Peter knew who to cry out to. Look below to see how Jesus responded.

"IMMEDIATELY Jesus reached out his hand and caught him." Matthew 14:31

I separated out this verse because it is just so awesome. Immediately—without lapse of time, without delay, instantly, at once—Jesus grabbed a hold of Peter and saved him from drowning. Jesus does the same for us.

In the storms of life, we may feel like we are drowning and that Jesus doesn't care but that is not truth. Jesus cares so deeply. He is reaching out His hand to save us. He promises to be with us in everything. He is with us in the storm. We will get through it. Wow... let that soak in.

Claim it.

Embrace it.

Believe it.

Take hold of Jesus' hand and trust that He will immediately be there with you and never let you go.

Heavenly Father, thank You for reaching out to save me in the storms of life. Thank You that You are an immediately God. Please help me to believe the truth that I am not drowning. You are with me every step of the way. Please teach me how to keep my eyes on You instead of the storm. I love You, LORD. In Jesus name, Amen.

—Anastasia

Today God is stirring my heart by...

I DARE YOU!

"My dear brothers and sisters, take note of this: Everyone should be quick to listen, slow to speak."

James 1:19

Listening—one of the hardest things to do. What does it mean to listen? Here is the definition taken from The Webster's dictionary: "to pay attention to someone in order to hear what is being said and understand that it is serious, important, or true."

When I read over this definition, I am convicted. How many times has a friend shared a concern with me and I haven't really listened to them? How do I listen for the benefit of my friend?

When I listen for the benefit of my friend, I am concentrating on paying attention in order to hear what is being said. I am hearing and understanding that what my friend is sharing is serious, important and very true to them. What they are dealing with is real. It's heavy on their heart. They are in the midst of it and just want to be heard. At times friends may want advice but more often than not they just want someone to listen. To validate. To encourage by just being there. To be heard. To have someone care.

Too often I have also been guilty of wanting to relate. When my friend shares about the hard day they are having, I want to share about mine too. After all, we all have things going on. We all have hard times. But, my friend is sharing because they need a listening ear. Unless they ask me to share what's happening with me, I am going to work on just listening. Just being there to encourage.

Another area that I really need to learn to listen is with my kids. They are growing so fast before my eyes. And if I don't stop and really listen to them, I am going to miss out on some pretty important moments. The other day my oldest daughter Micaela was telling me a story about her day. It was right in the middle of me getting dinner ready too. I had a choice to make in that moment. Would I stop and truly listen to my daughter's heart or would I keep going and half listen so I can get dinner in on time? I am learning more and more that I need to stop, look my kids in the eyes and listen to their heart. Ten years down the road I am going to care more about knowing my daughter than having dinner ready on time that day or any day for that matter.

I am committed to becoming a better listener with my husband, my kids and my friends. I don't want to miss out on really hearing them. So, how about you? How well do you listen to your spouse? To your friends? To your children? I dare you to just listen. And only listen! Like our key verse for today, let us be known as people who are quick to listen and slow to speak.

Heavenly Father, I want to be quick to listen and slow to speak. Please teach me how to really listen to others. I want to show others that they are valuable enough for me to stop and listen. And not just listen but support and encourage as needed. Please teach me to care about others like You do. Thank You, Jesus. In Jesus name, Amen.

—Anastasia

Today God is stirring my heart by…

JESUS SPEAKS

"[Jesus] took her by the hand and said to her, "Talitha koum!" (Which means "Little girl, I say to you, get up!"). Immediately the girl stood up and began to walk around (she was twelve years old). At this they were completely astonished."

Mark 5:41–42

Who is your favorite speaker of all time? What do you like about this person? When he or she speaks, do other people listen? Do they lean in to hear what is being said? There are many people in our lives that we admire and want to listen to. Back in Bible times, Jesus was one of those people. Crowds surrounded Jesus most of the time. They followed Jesus to hear Him speak. Why? Because Jesus spoke with authority. Mark 5 is filled with stories of how the voice of Jesus changed people.

The chapter begins with Jesus stepping out of a boat in the region of Gerasenes. A man who had an impure spirit within him came from the tombs to meet Jesus. This man lived in the tombs and no one could bind him anymore. Night and day, this man would cry out and cut himself with stones. How did this man get free? Jesus spoke. The very words of Christ had the power to tell the demons who possessed this man where to go. Jesus had the power to completely heal this man. Can you imagine the freedom this man felt? We don't know how many years this man was like that. But any amount of time would have been torture. Jesus stepped into a very hopeless situation, spoke and brought healing.

Jesus then crossed over to the other side of the lake. Soon after stepping out of the boat, he was approached by Jairus, a synagogue leader. Jairus' daughter was dying and he believed Jesus could heal her. So, Jairus asked Jesus to come and Jesus agreed.

On their way to Jairus' house, we encounter another healing. So many people pressed into Jesus as he moved along. At one point, Jesus felt power go out of Him. So, Jesus spoke and asked who touched Him. Jesus' disciples thought he was crazy. There were so many people crowding around Jesus. How could they possibly know? But, Jesus once again had spoken and ushered in healing by His voice. Jesus looked around to see who had done it. Finally, the women who had been bleeding twelve years came forward and told Jesus the truth. In Mark 5:34. Jesus responded "Daughter, your faith has healed you. Go in peace and be freed from your suffering." Jesus spoke hope and healing into another hopeless situation.

While Jesus was still talking, some people came up to Jairus and told him that his daughter was dead. In Mark 5:36, we read "Overhearing what they said, Jesus told him, "Don't be afraid; just believe." Jesus spoke and asked Jairus to trust Him. Soon they arrived at Jairus's house. Jesus went in with the girl's parents and His disciples. He walked over to the girl, took her by the hand and said *"Talitha koum!"* (Which means "Little girl, I say to you, get up!"). Immediately the girl stood up and began to walk around (she was twelve years old). At this they were completely astonished." The voice of Jesus once again brought hope and healing to a very hopeless situation.

Jesus loves to walk into very hopeless situations. He speaks life, hope and healing. Jesus brings incredible peace. What situation in life are you facing right now that feels hopeless? Friends, trust that Jesus can breathe life into your situation. Take a look back on your life to see how Jesus already has done this. Make a list to remind yourself of God's faithfulness. And keep believing for Jesus to breathe more life, hope and healing!

Heavenly Father, thank You for the many examples of how You breathed life into hopeless situations. I love that You cared so much for the demon possessed man, the women who had bled for twelve years and Jairus' daughter. Thank You for caring about every one of my needs. God, You are so good! Please help me to remember all the ways you have come through. Help me to trust that You will breathe life, hope and healing in my life. I love You, LORD. In Jesus name, Amen.

—Anastasia

Today God is stirring my heart by…

VICTORY IN JESUS

"Jesus said "I have told you these things, so that in me you may have peace. In this world you will have trouble. But take heart! I have overcome the world."

John 16:33

Facebook is a great tool to share about what's on our hearts and ask for prayer. But, we have to be careful how much attention we give to Satan in our posts. The other day, I was reading some posts on Facebook. I started to get so frustrated and bothered. I had to take a step back and ask Jesus why I was so bothered. The answer came fairly quickly. Many of the posts were focused on Satan attacking the person. It just burns me up inside when I see talk about "Satan this, and Satan that." As redeemed followers of Jesus Christ, we need to stop giving attention to Satan and start giving our attention, praise, and focus to JESUS!

I understand that Satan opposes us and it is good to understand that we are in a war. In Ephesians 6, we read about the armor of God and our need to put it on daily. In verses 12–13, we read "For our struggle is not against flesh and blood, but against the rulers, against the authorities, against the powers of this dark world and against the spiritual forces of evil in the heavenly realms. Therefore put on the full armor of God, so that when the day of evil comes, you may be able to stand your ground, and after you have done everything, to stand." We don't ever want to go into a war zone without the armor of God.

However, when we start talking about and focusing on Satan attacking us, it becomes another way that we become self-focused and promote a victim mindset. We will experience victory when we start declaring the truth of Jesus rather than the lie of Satan. Jesus has overcome and because of that we are overcomers! So instead of talking about what Satan has done, let's start talking about what God is doing! Jam to some worship music, start listing God's blessings, or encourage someone else. In John 16:33, Jesus said "I have told you these things, so that in me you may have peace. In this world you will have trouble. But take heart! I have overcome the world." Jesus didn't promise it would be easy but He did promise that He will be with us. Isn't it awesome to know that no matter what comes our way, we have victory in Jesus?

I am *not* saying we should never talk about our struggles. I *am* sorry for all that has happened this past week that has pulled you down, discouraged or hurt you. I am sorry for the sickness and hurting family members. We do need to share with another sister who will pray for us and challenge us to look to Jesus. Then we need to start speaking the truth and promises of God. We need to look expectantly for the good God is going to bring in our lives through whatever circumstance we face.

Let's put our focus back on Jesus. Let's turn our eyes to His power and strength. Let's praise our awesome God!

Heavenly Father, I am sorry for the ways I have taken the focus off of praising You. Even in the hard times, You are at work. Thank You that You will bring good out of what is intended to harm me. Thank you that You have overcome and because of that, I can have victory. Please help me to keep my focus on You alone. Help praise to be on my lips at all times. In Jesus name, Amen.

—Anastasia

Today God is stirring my heart by...

REMEMBER

*"Do you not know? Have you not heard? The L*ORD* is the everlasting God, the Creator of the ends of the earth. He will not grow tired or weary, and his understanding no one can fathom. He gives strength to the weary and increases the power of the weak. Even youths grow tired and weary, and young men stumble and fall; but those who hope in the L*ORD* will renew their strength. They will soar on wings like eagles; they will run and not grow weary, they will walk and not be faint."*

Isaiah 40:28–31

Each year we remember and celebrate the life of Jeremiah David, the baby we miscarried in 2007. He would have been born on February 29, 2008. Each year we purchase a yellow rose and a blue balloon to celebrate him. The kids get involved and love this special day. Here's our story of how we remember.

We purchase a yellow rose because it symbolizes joy, delight and freedom. Though our hearts still grieve the loss of our baby, we choose to have joy. We know that Jeremiah is in a much better place. He is experiencing so much delight and freedom in heaven. And for that we are so grateful.

Our kids take turns sending the balloon to Jeremiah. We gather as a family in the backyard. We talk about Jeremiah and how old he would have been. The kids are well aware that they have a brother in heaven. Micaela, our oldest, even writes about Jeremiah in her prayer journal. This is so precious to me.

Each year, one of the kids releases the balloon to Jeremiah. We stand there and watch it go to him until we can't see the balloon anymore. The joy on the kids' faces as they watch the balloon go up shows me that they understand Jeremiah's life is significant.

We don't know for sure the gender of our baby since I was two months along when we miscarried. My husband Jonathan and I both believe it was a baby boy. So we named our baby Jeremiah David. The reason we chose this name is because of the meanings. Jeremiah means "Yahweh has uplifted, Exalt the Lord" and David means "Beloved." Losing our baby was one of the toughest time in our lives. It was heartbreaking to go through. The prayers we prayed for the baby to be spared were not answered. It didn't make sense and it hurt. But, we know that God was with us through it all. He grieved with us and continues to comfort us as we remember. We always want to exalt the Lord and uplift His name no matter what trials may come. We felt God's love and wanted Jeremiah to know he was dearly loved no matter how much time we had. His life was precious. So, that is the reason we choose David as his middle name.

Each of our children has a life song. It's a song that we prayed and asked God to give us. The song represents the baby's life and speaks truth over them in the years to come. Each day of pregnancy, we sang this song over our baby in the womb. God had given us Jeremiah's song, "Everlasting God." It is a song based on our key verses for today. It speaks powerful truth of praising God even in our heartache. These verses remind us that our strength is in God and He will renew us when we rest in His amazing power. This song has been a powerful tool in our healing.

One of the most precious gifts we received in our time of grief was a Willow Tree Angel. It is called Remember. My friend Angie who blessed us with this gift understood grief. She understood that no words can heal the hurt and she also knew the words to say to comfort us. She recognized that Jeremiah was indeed a life even though he didn't grow up outside of the womb. This is a gift I will always cherish.

To all the Moms who have lost a baby, I am so sorry. Your baby is a very precious life who is with Jesus now. Each year when we remember our baby, I pray for you too. My prayer is that as you remember, you will feel God's love surrounding and holding you close.

Heavenly Father, thank You for the gift of remembering. It is hard to experience loss at any level but I am so thankful You are with me. Thank You for the many ways You renew my strength. Help me to continually turn to You even in my heartache. I love You, LORD. In Jesus name, Amen.

—Anastasia

Today God is stirring my heart by...

ONENESS

"Wives, submit to your husbands as to the LORD. For the husband is the head of the wife as Christ is the head of the church, his body, of which he is the Savior. Now as the church submits to Christ, so also wives should submit to their husbands in everything. Husbands, love your wives, just as Christ loved the church and gave himself up for her to make her holy, cleansing her by the washing with water through the word, and to present her to himself as a radiant church, without stain or wrinkle or any other blemish, but holy and blameless. In this same way, husbands ought to love their wives as their own bodies. He who loves his wife loves himself."

Ephesians 5:22–28

Call me sentimental, but recently I celebrated my thirteen anniversary with my husband and I thought it fitting to spend some time in the Word studying about husbands, wives and this blessing (and yet really hard at times) called marriage! As I reflected, a few nuggets of truth came to mind…

#1: Love is a choice. It's not just a feeling, but a decision to love my husband even when I don't feel like it.

#2: I'm only responsible for myself. Wait. What? Yep, I can't control my husband's attitude, but I can control mine. I can't control how he responds to a situation or argument, but I can control how I do.

#3: My source of joy can't be found in my husband. When I

expect him, not God, to fill me with joy, I will always set him up for failure and I'll be disappointed.

#4: Change is inevitable. I'm a different person since I got married over a decade ago, and so is my husband. The key is to change together, to move in the same direction (together) instead of apart. How can we do that? Continue to be interested in what he is interested in, stay in the Word, keep open communication (with my husband and God), and don't be afraid of change but embrace it! BUT, and a big but, I can't change my husband, only God can.

#5: The best thing I can do for my kids is show and tell them how much I love their father. By being a great example to them of a healthy, loving, respectful marriage and to also give them reassurance.

So what does God say about marriage? What better place to start than at the beginning with Adam and Eve in Genesis 2:18, 20–23. "The Lord God said, 'It is not good for the man to be alone. I will make a helper suitable for him.' But for Adam no suitable helper was found. So the Lord God caused the man to fall into a deep sleep; and while he was sleeping, he took one of the man's ribs and closed up the place with flesh. Then the Lord God made a woman from the rib he had taken out of the man, and he brought her to the man. The man said, 'This is now bone of my bones and flesh of my flesh; she shall be called woman for she was taken out of man.'"

I love God's creativeness in illustrating the symbol of marriage by becoming one flesh. As husband and wife we were created and equipped for different tasks, but all these lead to the same goal— honoring God. When we become one with our husband it doesn't mean that we lose our personality or cover up who we are. Instead, it means caring for him as you care for yourself, putting his needs before your own and helping him become the person God desires for him to be.

God also says in Genesis 2:24 "For this reason a man will leave his father and mother and be united to his wife, and they will become one flesh." I found these words three times throughout the Bible as I was studying. I think God was trying to get his point across. I think of this verse and how it amplifies an oneness of marriage. As I kept reading this verse over and over it made me think that it's not only physical, but emotional as well. I cannot have oneness with my husband if I am sharing things about myself to others, but not to him. I cannot have oneness with my husband if I am constantly seeking counsel from others, but not from him. I cannot have oneness with my husband if I am giving so much to others, but not as much to him. I cannot have oneness with my husband when

I desire more for myself than for him.

Do any of these statements ring true to you? Ask God to show you an area in your life where you are creating a wall to be formed between you and your husband. And if you are not married, it doesn't hurt to start preparing your heart now. I often find it takes God days, months, or years to prepare me for what He has in store for me next.

Heavenly Father, thank You for creating this wonderful gift of marriage. The perfect example of how You love the church, You have asked that I love my husband. Work in me today to help identify the areas in which I am lacking. Bring unity between me and my husband and help me to knock down any walls I have begun to build that has caused our oneness to be split. In Jesus name, Amen.

—Natalie

Today God is stirring my heart by…

A COUPLE OF SANDWICHES

"The King will reply, 'Truly I tell you, whatever you did for one of the least of these brothers and sisters of mine, you did for me."

Matthew 25:40

My son Caleb and I were out running many errands one morning. We arrived at our destination so I unloaded Caleb from the van to head into the store. At the head of our van, a younger man softly said "Excuse me, do you have some food to give to a hungry person?" At first, I didn't quite catch what he said because I was a little fearful. Here I am with my 3 year old son being approached by a man. Now mind you, he had a smaller build and I could probably have defended myself, but still it bothered me. This young man was kind enough to stay further away from us so I relaxed a bit. He repeated his question. I responded that no, I didn't have any food and I moved on. The young man moved to the next person.

As I walked away, I felt bad. I really wished I had food in the van to give him. Growing up in the city, my Dad always taught me to be careful of people who ask for money. The best thing was to get a person some food. I would have loved to get this young man some food. I decided to just pray for him since I could do that.

It was at that moment that God whispered to my heart, "You have the lunch you packed for Caleb and you. You could give him that." I wish I could tell you that I said Yes to God right away. Instead, I argued a little bit. "But God I won't have a lunch to eat and we are a ways from home. And what about Caleb? He is 3 and he needs to eat." God gently nudged me and asked me to obey.

I went back and saw the young man. I told him that I remembered I had some sandwiches I had packed. I unloaded them and handed them over. He was very appreciative and walked towards another vehicle. I glanced back because honestly I thought maybe he was an angel in disguise. He was still there moving around the parking lot.

God whispered to my heart, "It doesn't matter what he does with your sandwiches. What matters is that you obeyed." I am so glad I turned around and listened to God. My steps felt lighter as I headed into the store.

Lunchtime got closer and closer as we finished up our errands. When I felt the hunger pains, I spent time praying for that young man's needs to be met. As we loaded up after our last errand, Caleb was asking for his lunch. I reminded him what we did with our lunch. I talked about how God asked me to give it to the man and I obeyed. Caleb responded with "Oh yeah Mommy. Jesus can help that man." My heart was full.

My little man Caleb knew that God would provide for this man. I am honored that God chose me. Even though I didn't obey right away and even argued a bit, I feel good about obeying in the end. It was another step in becoming more aware of those around me and how I can be Jesus to them.

Who needs you to be Jesus to them today?

Heavenly Father, thank You for using me despite myself. Please help me to be more aware of those around me. Please continue to use me to bless Your children. God, I want to say yes right away. Help me to walk in obedience each step of the way. I love You,, Jesus. In Jesus name, Amen.
—Anastasia

Today God is stirring my heart by…

HANDPRINT

"Let those who fear the LORD say; 'His love endures forever.' In my anguish I cried to the LORD, and he answered by setting me free."

Psalm 118:4–5

Each year when the warmer weather comes, I burst in excitement to work in my landscaping. After a long winter, it brings me joy to get my hands in the dirt and prep my plants for the new season. And most years, my track record usually concludes with a bad sunburn, even after applying sunscreen. Three years ago as I lathered myself up with sunscreen, instead of washing my hand, I patted my back to wipe it off… and then forgot to apply sunscreen to my back. I'm sure you can imagine where this story is going. Oh yes. I burnt horribly, except for one spot on my back. Yep! A big ole handprint. And ladies, let me just tell you, I get deathly pale during the winter. If pale was a crayon color, they would name it Natalie. So imagine a bright red back with a shockingly *white* handprint. I tried everything to get rid of it. At one point I even put on sunscreen all around the handprint and then tried to burn it. Nope, the little stinker would not change color at all. So from April until October I had a handprint on my back. Seriously, you can't make this stuff up.

As I look back at that summer, I realized I couldn't get away from my mistake. Every day was a reminder that I messed up. And isn't that what Satan wants to do to us? Mentally beat ourselves down over and over from our mistakes, our shortcomings, our failures. Not God. He tells us in Isaiah 1:18 "Come now, and let us reason together," Says the LORD, "Though your sins are like scarlet, they shall be as white as snow; though they are red like crimson, they shall be as wool."

Does anyone else see the same color scheme as my handprint? Oy! Satan wants to keep us in bondage—God wants to give us freedom. Satan wants us to feel condemned—God wants us to feel redeemed. Satan wants us to live a life of regrets—God wants us to live a life of promises. You don't have to walk around anymore "marked" by your sins and mistakes. Ask for forgiveness, allow God to cleanse you from them, and then by God's grace move on white as snow!

Heavenly Father, I'm so thankful that I serve the one true God that doesn't hold my mistakes over my head. Once I confess them to You, they are gone. In You I can find my value, in You I find redemption, and in You I find my eternal salvation. In Jesus name, Amen.

—Natalie

Today God is stirring my heart by…

WATCH
YOUR WORDS

"She speaks with wisdom, and faithful instruction is on her tongue."

Proverbs 31:26

Do you like to people watch? Do you ever try to guess what their life is like? You can learn a lot about a person by watching them. You can also learn a lot about yourself. The other day was one of those days that I learned a lot.

I was enjoying my soft pretzel while watching people in line. One family in particular jumped out at me. It was a Mom and her two daughters. Their shoulders were slumped and they were anxious to eat. As they discussed what they were getting, the Mom growled "We are only getting one strawberry shake and you will share it." The girls didn't accept the answer very well which only escalated the Mom's anger. I looked down at my food and tried to block out their conversation.

A few minutes later, I looked up at the cashier when I heard some laughter. Guess who I saw? That same Mom! She was so kind and light hearted with the cashier. Her countenance had totally changed. After paying and walking off to the side, I could see the irritation come out. I once again watched the older daughter shrink before my eyes. The words her Mom spoke to her probably felt justified but weren't necessary. The sadness in the girl's eyes was so evident and I really wanted to reach out to her.

In that moment, the Holy Spirit whispered to my heart. "Aren't you just like that Mom sometimes?" I was challenged, convicted and found myself repenting. In fact, just yesterday, I lost my cool with my son in public all because he asked the same question twice. Was that really necessary? No.

I felt that Mom's irritation and frustration because I have been there. She reminded me so much of myself. I let kid's behaviors or attitudes get to me too much. They annoy me and then I react in frustration or anger. I feel justified in how I act. But, in reality, I need to be watching my words and attitude with my kids. I need to respond in love and have faithful instruction.

Would I talk to the cashier the same way I just talked to my kids? No way! Then, why do I think I have the right to talk to my kids that way? I would much rather kids get the side of me that is pleasant. I would much rather be known to my kids as a kind, loving, and patient person.

How about you? Do you watch your words?

Heavenly Father, I need You to help me watch my words. I want my children to get my best and speak to them as I would speak to a cashier. When I open my mouth, I want to speak with wisdom and have faithful instruction on my tongue. Holy Spirit, please guide me. Help me to hold my tongue when I need to. Please help me love with my words. In Jesus name, Amen.

—Anastasia

Today God is stirring my heart by…

A HUMBLING PERSPECTIVE

"This is what the LORD says: "Heaven is my throne, and the earth is my footstool. Where is the house you will build for me? Where will my resting place be? Has not my hand made all these things, and so they came into being?" declares the LORD. "This is the one I esteem: he who is humble and contrite in spirit, and trembles at my word."

Isaiah 66: 1–2

Humble is not a word we hear very often in our society, but when we are dished up a big piece of it, boy do we understand it! A couple years ago I started my dreaded monthly cycle a few days early and I was not prepared. So at eight o'clock in the morning, I walked into the one store in my tiny town where everyone knows your name, dressed in flannel pajamas, no make-up—and yes, I did manage to put a bra on—to purchase my needed items. Ten minutes later I had three large boxes of tampons, a package of could-soak-up-a-flood-if-need-be pads, a box of mozzarella sticks and a big bottle of Coke to wash down my sorrows—there is no judgment here, right? I got up to the check-out counter and of course the cashier was a guy. Awkward. Like the kind of awkward where if we made eye contact we both looked away immediately. Ah, but thankfully nothing so horrible that a mozzarella stick couldn't fix.

Walking out of the store, I had to wonder how much being humble plays a vital role in keeping our perspective. When we are being self-centered, putting ourselves before others, and keeping our eyes on *our* needs, *our* struggles and *our* desires (do you see a pattern here?), we leave very little room to be humble. God tells us *twice* in James 4:6 and in 1 Peter 5:5, "God opposes the proud but gives grace to the humble." I think He's pretty serious about getting His point across.

The definition of humble reads: having or showing a modest or low estimate of one's own importance. I think in a spiritual definition, humbling ourselves means that we recognize our worth comes from God. Being humble means we work with God and in His power. Being humble is realizing we don't deserve His grace or favor in our life. Being humble means we give reverence to God's Word and respect His message on how we are to live our lives. In turn, we view things through His eyes—which will give us the perspective that we need. What better point of view to have than God's.

Heavenly Father, You have promised in Your word when I humble myself before You that You will lift me up. Humble my heart and mind so that I am better able to focus on what really matters. In Jesus name, Amen.

—Natalie

Today God is stirring my heart by…

PUNCHING THE WAVES

"The LORD is my light and my salvation—whom shall I fear? The LORD is the stronghold of my life—of whom shall I be afraid?"

Psalm 27:1

What is he doing? I can't tell if he is laughing or crying. From my spot on the blanket, I observed Nathan in the big waves. Earlier in the day, he had been so scared to go out in the water by himself. So, I was very surprised he was out there. I spent a little more time watching him and came to the conclusion that he was laughing.

With my camera in hand, I moved as close as I could without disturbing Nathan. He was jumping at the big waves and punching them. The excitement and laughter was contagious. Wave after wave, he punched and laughed. I found myself punching with him. His chest grew bigger and he stood taller. Nathan was conquering the waves instead of letting the waves conquer him.

What brought about this change? About a half hour before this, Nathan had spent time with his Daddy in the waves. He grabbed hold of his Daddy's hand and faced the waves. Nathan wasn't alone in the waves. His Daddy had protected him. Nathan's Daddy had taught him how to work with the waves. He was able to punch the waves all because he spent time with his Dad.

In that moment, God whispered to my heart. He reminded me of the many waves of life I had conquered because of spending time with him. God reminded me of how different I am when I have spent time with Him. As I sat and reflected, I realized that I do always feel stronger after my daily time with God. I do feel like I can conquer anything that comes my way. I have learned to hold tight to my Daddy's hand and relax because He is in control. My time with my heavenly Daddy changes me. I am stronger. I'm ready to go punch some large waves and laugh as I do so.

I loved the way that Nathan was transformed because of spending time with his Daddy. We can be transformed too. Each time we read the Bible, God can speak into our hearts. Anytime we take time to pray and listen, God can teach us so many things.

How about you? How do you feel after spending time with Jesus? Do you feel equipped to punch the waves of life? God wants to pour His wisdom and strength into you. Will you let God do that each day?

Heavenly Father, thank You for the ways You strengthen me and fill me when I spend time with You. I am transformed by being with You. Please help me to continue to spend time in Your word and in prayer. Thank You for equipping me to punch the waves of life. In Jesus name, Amen.

—Anastasia

Today God is stirring my heart by…

GOD
KNOWS YOU

"Oh Lord, you have searched me and you know me. You know when I sit and when I rise; you perceive my thoughts from afar. You discern my going out and my lying down; you are familiar with all my ways. Before a word is on my tongue you know it completely, O Lord."

Psalm 139: 1–4

One night as I brushed out my mane… I mean hair… I couldn't believe how much hair fell out. It was one of those many times I stopped and said in shock, "How am I not bald yet?" As I pulled a fist full of thousands of hairs out (slight exaggeration), I thought to myself—how many hairs have I lost today? Then in God's still small voice I hear, *"I know. I know the number of hairs you lost and the number that is still on your head. I know you well. I know the good that overflows from your heart because I put it there. I know what makes you laugh, what makes you cry, and what makes you scared. I know your insecurities, your hopes, your desires and your needs. I know that you yelled at your kids today, put yourself before your husband and didn't spend much time with me—and I still love you."*

I don't know about you, but God's love for me is quite humbling. The God of the universe knows everything about us—the good, the bad, and the ugly—and still loves us. Some days I am so overwhelmed by God's great, unconditional, and pure love for us. He cares about every detail of our life. He heals us physically, emotionally and mentally. He spared us from darkness and death. I think David writes it well in Psalm 103: 1–5, "Praise the LORD, O my soul, all my inmost being, praise his holy name. Praise the LORD, O my soul, and forget not all his benefits—who forgives all your sins and heals all your diseases, who redeems your life from the pit and crowns you with love and compassion, who satisfies your desires with good things so that your youth is renewed like the eagles."

Do you ever struggle with God's love for you? Do you hold back from God because you feel you don't deserve his love? No one deserves it, that's what makes His unending pursuit after us that much more amazing. When we draw near to God, He draws near to us.

Heavenly Father, thank You for loving a sinner like me and wanting the very best for me, even when I don't deserve it. You love me not because of what I have or haven't done, but just because I am Yours. Thank you for knowing everything about me, and loving me unconditionally anyway. In Jesus name, Amen.

—Natalie

Today God is stirring my heart by…

WHILE IT WAS STILL DARK

"Very early in the morning, while it was still dark, Jesus got up, left the house and went off to a solitary place, where he prayed."

Mark 1:35

What does your prayer life look like? Do you take time daily to pray? Do you pray throughout the day? Do you look forward to your time talking to God? Over the years my prayer life has changed. As I take more and more time to pray, I have learned time and time again of the importance of talking to my Daddy.

My greatest example has been Jesus. It amazes me that the Son of God, the Savior of the World, took time to pray. Jesus knows everything. He knows the beginning to the end. Yet, Jesus also knew the importance of taking time to talk to His Daddy. Jesus knew the source of all His strength. He knew that He had to surrender to God's will before the day even began.

I can learn so much from Jesus. He began His day by getting up and going straight to God. Jesus took time to get away from the busyness and demands of life. He took time to talk with His Daddy to build the most important relationship. How do you start your day? As Moms, we always have something going. Depending on the season of life we are in, we may only have a few minutes to talk to God. Any amount of time you can talk to God is investing in your relationship with Him. So, follow Jesus' example and take it when you can get it.

The other thing I learn about Jesus is that He knew the source of all His strength. Jesus knew He couldn't face the day without tapping into God's power. Yes, Jesus is fully God, but He was human on earth. He needed to depend on God's supernatural strength. Do you depend on God for strength? Or do you depend on yourself and end up running dry? You will never run out of God's strength. Take time the time for a fill up each morning like Jesus did.

The final thing I learn from Jesus in this verse is that I must take time to surrender to His will for my day. Too often, I plow into my day with a long list of to do's. I'm ready to conquer the world and knock out anything that stands in my way. It's not a bad thing to be motivated or have a plan. But, too often our plans change or something or someone gets in our way. When we take the time to surrender our day to God each morning, the interruptions turn into divine appointments because we have the eyes to see how God is working.

God longs for us to be like Jesus. He desires us to pause and take time away from the busyness of life. God wants a relationship with us. He also desires to fill us up with more than enough strength to face whatever comes our way. Will you surrender to God's will for your day? I promise that you will have a better day!

Heavenly Father, I love that Jesus came to You each day. If Jesus needed to do that, I know I definitely need it. God, I want to be filled up with Your strength instead of my own. I desire to surrender my day to You and long for Your will. Thank You for caring so deeply about me. In Jesus name, Amen.

—Anastasia

Today God is stirring my heart by…

BE PROUD TO REPRESENT

"For you were once darkness, but now you are light in the
LORD. Live as children of light (for the fruit of the light
consists in all goodness, righteousness and truth) and find
out what pleases the LORD."

Ephesians 5: 8–10

My husband loves to wear masks and wigs. He thinks it's hilarious. President heads, an old man, a gorilla, an Angry Bird, a bad 70's hippy wig and an afro are all in his collection. Well, once a year my husband takes our boys on a weekend camping trip with some other dads and their boys and on one of these trips he thought it would be fun to spice up the road trip a bit. So what does my husband do? Well, he of course puts on the gorilla mask to drive. Another dad took a picture of him doing this and posted it on Facebook and tagged him.

At little side note: This was right around the time I had my first book published. Because you can't make this stuff up—the very first comment on the picture was, "Replogle. I just bought a book by someone with the name of Replogle. Is there any relation?" The next comment below by the picture taker wrote, "Is the book by Natalie Replogle? If so, that's her husband." Oh my goodness! Needless to say, it has become quite the joke at our house as I tease my husband over the incident with, "Babe, you have to represent me now. I can't represent the Replogle name all by myself!"

As I think about this story and continually laugh about how

everything played out, my thoughts turned to think about the word "represent." We as believers represent the one True King. We are to go out into the world and represent the God that loves without finding fault, forgives continually, gives grace mercifully, shows kindness, and speaks justly. I don't know about you, but I have on many occasions not represented the LORD like I should have.

How did you represent God in the last week with your family? Did you give the best representations of who God is to your children? Did you represent God in the words you spoke to your friends? Did the love you showed your husband represent Christ's love? Did your actions and reactions this past week give a testimony to the God we serve?

Each day we need to walk with our head held high because we have been given the great honor to represent our God. May we never take this responsibility lightly or for granted. Jesus tells us with His own words in Matthew 5:16 "Let your light shine before men, that they may see your good deeds and praise your Father in Heaven."

Heavenly Father, I haven't represented You as well as I should have lately. Help me to keep You in my forethoughts so that my first instinct is to always better Your Kingdom. In Jesus name, Amen.

—Natalie

Today God is stirring my heart by...

SHOW ME

"Show me your ways, LORD, teach me your paths."

Psalm 25:4

Have you ever been stuck somewhere? And then you tried and tried to get yourself unstuck without any success. Me too. It's not a fun feeling. The struggle is real. But all too often, I feel like we set ourselves up for struggles instead of success. God used my niece to teach me a lesson about that the other day.

My sister, my daughters and niece all arrived at home after a fun shopping outing. We were tired and ready to eat. So, after putting the car in park, we all started to unbuckle and hop out. I noticed my niece Annabelle was struggling to get out of her seat. The way she was trying to get out of the vehicle was blocked by bags and other items. I encouraged her to go the other way since it was wide open. There were no obstacles in her way and she could have easily gotten out. Annabelle looked over to the other side and debated. She decided to keep trying to get out the challenging side. Finally, she was able to get out.

I have to admit I was quite impressed with Annabelle. She is a determined young lady. Annabelle persevered until she could get herself out of the vehicle. We can learn a lot from my niece from this experience.

First, focusing on an end goal is important. It keeps us going and gives us a purpose. Like Annabelle, we can develop perseverance in whatever we find ourselves facing. In her instance, she wanted to get out of the car. In our lives, we can keep our focus on Jesus and trust His plan in any circumstance we find ourselves facing.

Secondly, determination is a great skill to have. When we set our mind to something, no matter what obstacles come our way, we can keep pressing on. Annabelle was very determined. She wanted out of that vehicle and her determination was rewarded.

This experience can also teach us that we need to ask God which way is best. Too often, we try to go our own way. We think we know what is best. The path we are walking down may be filled with struggle. Sometimes we bring on this struggle on ourselves because we have decided to go our own way instead of God's way. Our key verse for today is great to pray daily and sometimes throughout the day. I would much rather go God's way that is clear instead of the way I think is best.

God used Annabelle to teach me many things that day. I want to be a person who is focused, determined and surrendered. I want to ask God daily what His ways are. I want to be in the Word searching out God's heart for my life. Will you join me in this? Will you become a person who is focused, determined and surrendered?

Heavenly Father, I want to be a person who is focused, determined and surrendered. I want to focus on You and Your plan for my life. I want to be determined and give my all to whatever you call me to. Jesus, please teach even more how to surrender my life to Your ways. I want to know Your ways. Please show me. Thank You LORD. In Jesus name, Amen.

—Anastasia

Today God is stirring my heart by…

PREPARE FOR
BATTLE

"Finally, be strong in the LORD and in his mighty power.
Put on the full armor of God so that you can take your
stand against the devil's schemes. For our struggle is not
against flesh and blood, but against the rulers, against the
authorities, against the powers of this dark world and
against the spiritual forces of evil in the heavenly realms.
Therefore put on the full armor of God, so that when the
day of evil comes, you may be able to stand your ground,
and after you have done everything to stand. Stand firm
then, with the belt of truth buckled around your waist,
with the breastplate of righteousness in place, and with
your feet fitted with the readiness that comes from the
gospel of peace. In addition to all this, take up the shield
of faith, with which you can extinguish all the flaming
arrows of the evil one. Take the helmet of salvation and
the sword of the Spirit, which is the word of God. And
pray in the Spirit on all occasions with all kinds of prayers
and requests. With this in mind, be alert and always keep
on praying for all the saints."

Ephesians 6:10–18

About fifteen years ago I used to be a missionary in Ecuador and taught English to a bunch of elementary kids. I had a one of a kind, awesome experience and each day I am thankful that I stepped out in obedience and went when God called. But let me tell you, I used to have some terrible, horrible, no good, very bad days. I would constantly be sick, I had language barriers, I missed my family and friends, and most days the kids were very difficult to teach.

These verses above became my lifeline. I had them memorized and claimed them over me each morning. Recently, God brought this back to my mind and I realized how I've slipped in this area. I began to wonder how different my days would go if I started each and every day declaring these verses over me. When my feet touch the ground in the morning, I have entered a battle field. God has already promised us victory, but we will engage in struggles until He returns. The enemy's entire goal is to pull us away from God, bring us back to sin, and give sin a foothold in our lives.

The best way to defend ourselves is to put on our armor every day. Satan wants to tell us lies, God tells us to put on the belt of truth. Satan wants us to walk in wickedness, God tells us to put on the breastplate of righteousness. Satan wants us to worry and to keep us captive with a war going on in our minds and lives, God tells us to have our feet fitted with the readiness that comes from the gospel of peace. Satan wants us to believe that God doesn't love us enough, won't help us, won't guide us and won't work in our lives, but God says to take up the shield of faith so we can extinguish all the flaming arrows of the evil one. Satan doesn't want us to spend time in the Word because he knows how powerful we will be, but God tells us to take the helmet of salvation (to guard our mind and thoughts) and the sword of the Spirit. Satan wants to catch us off guard, but God tells us to be alert and to always keep praying.

Reading this, I've decided that I've given the enemy too much domain in my life. How about you? I've also decided that I want to start clinging to these verses once again. I'm tired of stepping into battle unprepared. Satan's best time to attack us is when we are distracted, unprepared, and weak. In 1 Peter 5:8 (MSG) it says, "Keep a cool head. Stay alert. The Devil is poised to pounce, and would like nothing better than to catch you napping. Keep your guard up." The battle will come ladies, whether we are ready or not. Why not fight with everything we have!

Heavenly Father, too often I start my day unprepared for what lies ahead. I desire to win the battles that come my way and You have given me the tools to be victorious. Give me the power through your Holy Spirit each day to defeat the enemy. God, help me to seek Your truth and to have clarity when lies come my way. Give me a desire to seek righteousness and walk in Your ways with a pure heart. Pour Your peace over me so that when You direct me, I don't have to hesitate because I feel Your presence and which way You are calling me. Give me the confidence to walk out in faith in all areas of my life, big or small. Clear my mind as I read Your Word that I may soak up Your wisdom so that I am better able to defend myself against the evil one. Have Your Spirit rest in me so that I may always be alert and keep my eyes on You. In Jesus name, Amen.

—Natalie

Today God is stirring my heart by...

GO FOR THE WIN!

"I have hidden your word in my heart that I might not sin against you."

Psalm 119:11

Do you like to play hide and seek? Do you always try to find the best place so no one could find you? I loved the challenge to be the last one found. I would work hard to find the perfect spot. Sometimes it worked, sometimes it didn't. But you can bet I always tried.

When I read our key verse, I am reminded of my hide and seek days as a kid. This verse challenges me. Do I see it as a challenge to hide God's word in my heart? Do I think creatively and do all that I can to hide God's word in my heart? I have come to realize that when I hide God's word in my heart, I win every single time. How do I win in life? The 3 ways that I win when I hide God's word in my heart are conviction, comfort, and challenge.

Each day as I dig into God's word, I am convicted on some level. There are days where it's a little reminder. And then there are those days where God uses His word to convict me. In Proverbs 16:32, we read "Better a patient person than a warrior, one with self-control than one who takes a city." I just blew up at one of my children over something so small. Did I display self-control? Am I teaching my children how to have self-control when they are upset about something? I love how God uses His word to convict me. My goal in life is to be more like Jesus and if there is something in my character that is not lining up, I'm thankful when God calls me out on it.

God uses His word to comfort me. There are days where circumstances are tougher than others. It's in these times that I lean more heavily into the Word I have hidden in my heart. The more I spend time in the Word, the more I see God's heart for His children. He loves us so deeply and cares about everything we are going through. A few of my favorite verses that God uses to comfort me are: "The LORD will fight for you; you need only to be still."—Exodus 14:14 and "The LORD is Close to the brokenhearted and saves those who are crushed in spirit." –Psalm 34:18. There are so many more verses that God uses to bring comfort. In those times, I love having God's word in my heart to depend on.

One more way that I win by hiding God's word in my heart is that I am challenged. As I spend time in the word, I see how Jesus lived. I read stories of the Bible characters who stayed standing when asked to kneel to a statue, who went against all odds and knocked down a giant with a stone, and who saved a nation by going before the King uninvited. I am challenged to be more like Jesus. I am challenged to have the faith of a mustard seed. I am challenged to stand and trust God no matter what the circumstances look like.

You will win at life when you hide God's word in your heart. God will use His word to challenge, comfort, and convict you. Will you do your part and read His word daily? I promise that you will not be disappointed. God's word is powerful. God's word has stood the test of time. You can depend on it.

Heavenly Father, thank You for the gift of Your Word. Please help me to take time daily to hide Your Word in my heart. It will always be a win for me. Thank You for convicting, comforting, and challenging me with Your Word. I love You, LORD. In Jesus name, Amen.

—Anastasia

Today God is stirring my heart by...

WHAT'S THE POINT?

"Do not be deceived; God cannot be mocked. A man reaps what he sows. The one who sows to please his sinful nature, from that nature will reap destruction; the one who sows to please the Spirit, from the Spirit will reap eternal life. Let us not become weary in doing good, for at the proper time we will reap a harvest if we do not give up!"

Galatians 6: 7–9

Monday is my cleaning day—and it is quite an undertaking since I usually take Sundays off. I pick up the house, clean bathrooms, mop, vacuum, dust, and usually get all loads of laundry done for the week. I'm usually exhausted by the end of the day, but that's what works best for *me* and my schedule. Well, one Monday I had just finished mopping my kitchen floor and my daughter wanted a bowl of cereal for snack. You can guess where this is going. Yep, all over my spotless floor. I handled it *shockingly* well with gentleness (which is my focus this year because I could have so easily let gentleness be bulldozed over with a lot of yelling). But as I'm on my hands and knees scrubbing a ten-foot radius of debris, I'm asking God, "What's the point? Why am I working so hard to keep this house clean when everywhere I turn the kids are destroying it?"

Have you heard the quote, "Cleaning your house with children around is like brushing your teeth while eating Oreos?" I think that might be engraved on my headstone. Are you like me? Have you ever asked God, "What's the point?" Maybe there is someone in your life that you continually have to forgive. Maybe you have a sin you struggle with that you can't kick. Maybe your marriage is falling apart and it's hard to find hope. Maybe you have been praying for something for so long and it feels like a slap in the face by it going unanswered. Maybe, like me, the daily mundane is squeezing the life out of you.

What's the point? Why should we continue to do what's right and good? When I was on my knees in the middle of the kitchen, God reminded me in His still small voice that He promised, *He promised*, that at a proper time I will reap a harvest if I do not give up! We need to trust God for the results. We need to let His Spirit guide so that His kingdom is glorified. And we need to lean on Him when we are weary so that we can use His strength to continue.

Heavenly Father, You know my heart and You know which areas I need Your hope—to not give up. Give me guidance, comfort, healing and strength on the days I feel weak and wonder "What's the point?" You are the point LORD. Following and honoring you! In Jesus name, Amen.

—Natalie

Today God is stirring my heart by…

STEP OF FAITH

"I can do everything through Christ, who gives me strength."

Philippians 4:13

This morning I went for an eight mile run. It was a solid run and it felt amazing! To some people this sounds absolutely crazy. To others, it sounds impossible. It may feel like they could never run eight miles let alone a half mile. I used to think it was crazy and impossible too. Then God got a hold of my heart and asked me to step out in faith. Here is the story of how it all began…

In January of 2013, I attended the closing ceremony for a 40 day challenge the ladies were involved in at our church. As part of that time, we had to run upstairs, run around the track that is above our sanctuary, and come down to the stage. My first thought was "I'm not a runner, I don't want to do this. I'll just walk." But, the competitive spirit inside me burst through and I ran anyway. While running on that track, something came alive in me. It was awesome and I felt so free! It was in that moment that God stirred in my heart a desire to run. It was that day that He called me out and asked me to take a step of faith and start running.

I wish I could say I obeyed right away. I went back and forth with Him on it though. "Are you really sure you want me to run?" He always answered with a "Yes." I want to give you a little background so you understand my questioning a little more. I injured my right knee on a trampoline over 10 years ago. It healed up but then a couple years later, I reinjured it somehow. After going to doctors, having an MRI, and a seeing physical therapist, it was found that my knee cap doesn't track properly. This leads to inflammation and constant pain. Going up and down stairs can be unbearable sometimes. Over the past three years, I have received chiropractic care and now wear orthotics in my shoes to help with this pain. My doctor's recommended that running not be my main exercise. This became my excuse to run.

But, God had other plans. And I am so thankful He did! In July of 2013, I began my running journey. I started with the Couch to 5K program and used a running coach to help me with my form. It has been an amazing journey ever since.

You see, I never thought I would be a runner. But, here I am as a testimony that when God calls you to something, He will equip you. God will also provide amazing people along the way to cheer you on. My husband Jonathan has been my biggest fan and encouraged me so much to pursue running. I am forever grateful for his support.

I can honestly say I would not be the runner I am without my running buddies. They have challenged me, pushed me, encouraged me, have been with me through hard runs, and prayed for me as I battled an injury. My running friends have trained with me for my first half marathon and several of them took time out of their very busy lives to run it with me. I am who I am because of my awesome friends and running buddies.

Life is a lot like running. You need a coach. The ultimate coach, God, who knows all about you and calls you to step out in faith. You need a support system that will cheer for you along the way. You need people who will challenge you to go to the next level. You need friends who will pour into you and believe you can do it even when you feel like giving up.

What is God is calling you to do that seems impossible? I want to encourage you to go for it! He will be with you every step of the way. I am who I am because I chose to obey.

Here's to many more runs!

Heavenly Father, You are awesome. Thank You for calling me out to do the impossible. Please help me to dream big and truly believe that I can do anything because of Your strength. Thanks for empowering me each day. I love You, LORD.

—Anastasia

Today God is stirring my heart by...

WEATHER
THE STORM

"As he went along, he saw a man blind from birth. His disciples asked him, 'Rabbi, who sinned, this man or his parents, that he was born blind?' 'Neither this man nor his parents sinned,' said Jesus, 'but this happened so that the work of God might be displayed in his life.'"

John 9:1–3

Everyone has dealt with suffering at some point. Maybe you have just walked through it. Maybe you are in the midst. Some days the pain is almost too much to bear. Some days it's easy to lay it at Jesus' feet. Our sufferings are not meant to make us weak, but to build us up, teach us, give us insight, and strengthen our faith. Many times through my struggles I ask God, "Please don't let me be the same at the end. Change me. Mold me. Strengthen me. And help me not to go through this and miss what you are trying to teach me!"

Paul tells us in Romans 5:3–4, "Not only so, but we also rejoice in our sufferings, because we know that suffering produces perseverance; perseverance, character; and character, hope." Rewind back eight years ago and you wouldn't recognize that Natalie—and it went so much deeper than the sweatpants and no make-up every single day! My second child, Brayden, had sleeping problems (and I use that phrase loosely—I think it could be used as a means of torture). For the first two years of his life, he was up screaming for hours almost every night. On top of that, my husband was gone on many business trips (he's a pilot). Then Brayden got infected with a very serious and life threatening disease. During which I had two very difficult miscarriages. I was exhausted physically, mentally, and emotionally. I had nothing left to give to my family, friends, and especially God.

That was a very dark time for me and I often cringe when I walk down memory lane. But I stand as a witness that God refined me through that fire. I also stand serving a God that understands my pain. In Isaiah 53:3 it says, "He was despised and rejected by men, a man of sorrows, and familiar with suffering. Like one from whom men hide their faces he was despised, and we esteemed him not." Jesus understands physical pain, the loss of a loved one, and the deep wound of rejection. I don't know about you, but I never want to stand on the other side of my suffering and realize it was all in vain because I didn't let God work in and through me!

Through Paul's ministry he considered it a privilege to suffer for Christ. What better testimony can we give than our strengthened faith, trust in God, strong character, deeper compassion and the work of God in our lives?

Heavenly Father, today I'm really hurting. I feel alone and as if no one understands my struggles. But you do. As you comfort me LORD, help me to turn my eyes off of myself and on to You. Give me hope, when I feel hopeless. Speak Your truth when I believe the lies. Guide my life when I feel lost. And take this broken heart and heal it. In Jesus name, Amen.

—Natalie

Today God is stirring my heart by...

LET'S GO
TO THE MOON

"Joshua told them, "Don't hold back. Don't be timid. Be strong! Be confident!"

Joshua 10:25a, MSG

When is the last time you took a trip to the moon? For our family it was this afternoon. We really enjoyed our adventure on the moon. The weather was perfect. The kids LOVE going to the moon! What started as a random idea has turned into something very special for our kids.

Last summer, I asked my kids to get on their sunglasses, helmets and prepare their rocket ships for takeoff. I let them know we were going to the Moon. They looked at me like I was crazy. My oldest even commented "This is so boring!" without even knowing what was next. I remember thinking "Maybe this is a crazy idea." But, I pushed through my own resistance and comments from my kids and went ahead with my idea. 3, 2, 1 blast off!

We all landed safely on the moon. We stepped carefully out of our spaceships and looked over the moon. The Moon is our subdivision. It's large circle area that is almost a half mile around. In the center, there is tall grass and wildflowers.

We imagined what it would be like to live on the moon. The kids shared what they thought we would eat and activities we could do. Next, we loaded back into our rocket ships and circled the Moon several times. The kids had a blast that day and have talked about it ever since.

Since that day we have gone to the moon several times. The kids love to tell their friends about the Moon. Our kids have a sense of ownership now. Anytime we go by that area, the kids ask "When can we go to the moon?" They also exclaim about the changes being made to the Moon. There are now four homes on that land.

In our key verse for today, Joshua is encouraging his men in the middle of a war. With God's help, they had just conquered many of their enemies. Joshua was telling his men not to be afraid of the five kings. He didn't want them to be timid but instead strong and move forward to take care of these kings. Joshua encouraged his men to be confident. As parents, I feel like God is communicating the same thing to us: "Don't hold back. Don't be timid. Be strong! Be confident!" Even when our ideas seem silly or the kids complain, we need to be confident in our abilities as parents. We need to continue to rely on the creator of our children for wisdom in this journey of parenting.

I am so glad I pushed through my own resistance and the kids comments that day. We all would have missed out on so much. And now we have a new tradition. So, how about you? What are some ways you can be more confident and strong in your parenting? What adventure will you go on today with your kids?

Heavenly Father, thank You for the many ways You help me as a parent. Would You please grow my confidence as a parent? Please help me to push through my kids' resistance and go on adventures to build family identity. Thank You for making me a strong and confident parent. In Jesus name, Amen.

—Anastasia

Today God is stirring my heart by…

DON'T ASSUME

"A fool finds no pleasure in understanding but delights in airing his own opinions."

Proverbs 18:2

Back when my son was just an infant, we had so many health issues with him. He had a sleeping problem where he spent hours up at night screaming, along with hours of crying during the day. Around six months of age, he began to have some breathing issues on top of everything. We went to the doctor and found out he had infant asthma and needed to be on breathing treatments. Which isn't a huge deal... unless you haven't slept in six months and you were just handed the straw that broke the camel's back.

When I got to the equipment place to pick up everything I needed, I hit my breaking point. I sat in the chair to work with the employee... and I completely lost it. Ladies, calling it the "ugly cry" doesn't even begin to describe it. I couldn't form any words. Just cried and cried and cried. The older woman's eyes widen and she rushed around her desk, getting on her knees beside me and said, "Are you alright? Is it your husband? Is he hurting you?" WHAT? Oh my word, if I hadn't been such a hot mess I would have started laughing. Bless her heart.

Doesn't assuming add so much more drama to our lives? When we assume, we use our own opinion for what others are thinking. God even warns us of this in our scripture—"A fool finds no pleasure in understanding but delights in airing his own opinions." Assuming causes miscommunication in our relationships. More often than not, when we assume, we don't give people the benefit of the doubt. Many times our assumptions can turn into judgment. We assume why someone is doing something, saying something, acting a certain way or how they *will* handle a situation. We assume we know how people should handle things, without even walking a day in their shoes.

So how can we change this? We need to go to the source. We need to stop answering our own questions. And most importantly, we need to keep our eyes on Jesus. When we focus on Him, the answers we so desperately seek probably won't matter as much anymore!

Heavenly Father, You are the way, the truth and the life. Send forth Your light and Your truth, let them guide me; let them bring me to Your holy mountain, to the place where you dwell. (Psalm 43:3) In Jesus name, Amen.

—Natalie

Today God is stirring my heart by...

BOUNDARIES
ARE GOOD

"The boundary lines have fallen for me in pleasant places; surely I have a delightful inheritance. I will praise the LORD, who counsels me; even at night my heart instructs me. I keep my eyes always on the LORD. With him at my right hand, I will not be shaken."

Psalm 16:6–8

Have you ever received a text from a good friend and been irked by it? And maybe a little hurt. Okay, so you may have been hurt a lot. What have you learned from that text? Several months ago, I received one of those texts from one of my very best friends. I had been suffering from post-concussion headaches and really struggling physically and emotionally. God used this friend's text to change the course of my life. Literally.

In this text, my friend shared the above verses with me accompanied by a few thoughts that are what God used to rock my world. First, she shared that God has set up my boundaries and that they are good. I was mad because I felt like she was saying that God caused my concussion to happen. I also felt that my friend was telling me that I just needed to get over it. I had to take a step back and realize that my friend was not out to hurt me and that is not what she was trying to communicate to me.

You see, I grew up with a pattern that when I got physically got hurt or emotionally hurt, my parents would literally say to me "Quit crying. You're feeling sorry for yourself when you cry." So I learned that my hurt wasn't valid or what I was going through wasn't valid. This is a pattern I have noticed and am working with God to renew my mind on. It's so ingrained and obviously reared up when I read that line in my friend's text.

And then the part about God setting up these boundaries. I also really wrestled with that. I don't feel like He set these boundaries up. They were in place because of my injury. I wouldn't have them if I wasn't hurt. Another thought my friend shared from her own personal experience was "I am not a victim as I sometimes have felt." I thought my friend was telling me I was a victim. Again, my grid from growing up was what I was hearing this all through. So, I pressed into God and asked Him why this upset me so bad. I cried out to Him saying "I don't want these boundaries. They aren't good. I wouldn't be with these boundaries if it wasn't for this injury. I'm not acting like a victim. This was all an accident." I wrestled with God on this because often when something really upsets us, God has something for us in it.

I just love how God tenderly and patiently moves us along. He spoke to my heart and asked me to look at my attitude about my limits. Honestly, I was fighting the limits (boundaries). They didn't seem fair. I was limited to about 15 minutes of screen time at a time due to my concussion. This whole injury was an accident. Why do I have to deal with this? In all this, God brought me to a place that showed me that my limits are good. I can't heal without limiting myself. It will physically not come if I don't implement these limits. He also showed me that 15 minutes really is a long time. I CAN get a lot done in that amount of time. Instead of sulking about the allotted time, I need to use it well and be a good steward of that time.

In all this, God also brought to mind that I do have a victim mindset. Again, I wrestled with this. Really God? He showed me that the pattern I grew up with and is ingrained into me is a victim mindset. As I leaned into God, He started showing me ways that I do act like a victim. Wow! Crazy how I didn't realize it. I'm amazed and so thankful God is calling me out. It's tough to break habits that are ingrained but I know that with God, it can be done.

I love how God used my friend that day to start a BIG work in my heart. I am so thankful this friend was bold enough to listen to God and text me her thoughts. As you can clearly see, it changed my life. I love having friends who care about me being more like Jesus and that push me to grow.

So, the text time you receive a text that really bothers you, take a step back and ask God what He wants to teach you through it. Then, lean into God and listen to how He wants to use what is being said. Open your heart and let God change you from deep within. And make sure you thank God for that amazing friend that He used.

Heavenly Father, thank You for using friends in my life to challenge me. Thank You that You care so much about me and want me to be more like You. God, I want to be open and let You speak into my life. Please help me to take a step back when something hurts me. Help me to lean into You and get Your insight before reacting out of my hurt. I love You, LORD. In Jesus name, Amen.

—Anastasia

Today God is stirring my heart by…

BECOMING A PRAYER WARRIOR

"Devote yourself to prayer, being watchful and thankful."

Colossians 4:2

Prayer is such an integral part of our relationship with Christ. Prayer draws us closer to the Holy Spirit, takes the focus off ourselves and onto God, helps us become like-minded with Christ, gives us the opportunity to praise God, express our thankfulness, ask for forgiveness for our sins, and we are able to share the very depth of our hearts (the good, the bad, and the ugly—God can take it!)

I'll be honest with you for a moment, I used to really struggle with prayer. It was very overwhelming to me. I felt very awkward when I prayed out loud, the prayer requests seemed unending and I just honestly struggled to find the time for it. One day I asked God to give me a burning passion for prayer. Did I miraculously achieve that passion immediately? No. But I can tell you God did a stirring in my heart that day. He showed me that prayer was like a muscle and the more I exercised it, the stronger it would become in my life. A lot of times I felt overwhelmed by prayer requests and couldn't keep them all straight and then I felt guilty that I told someone I would pray for them, and then I honestly forgot. So God showed me that instead of telling someone I would pray for them, I needed to stop right there and pray WITH them—or before I respond to a prayer request on social media, I pray first and then tell the person I just prayed for them. And you know what, the more I prayed out loud the easier it became, the more I had a passion to be a prayer warrior, and it became *natural* to talk to God all day long.

I don't know where you are in your prayer-life... maybe you relate to my story, OR maybe it's hard for you to pray to God because your heart isn't in the right place and He feels far away, maybe you've been hurt in the past by prayer from the answers you received, maybe you're afraid to talk to God, or maybe you feel that prayer won't change anything.

Let me encourage you. Prayer changes things—and it will change you! God cares about you and loves you deeply. He desires for you to come and just talk to Him. It doesn't have to be fancy or with eloquent words, just open up your heart to Him and share. He can take your hurt, your anger, your frustration, your sadness, your fears, your uncertainties... He just wants you to come to Him. There are no hoops for you to jump through, you don't have to come clean or perfect... He just wants you to come to Him.

When it comes to prayer, we also find joy in our communion with Him. Prayer is such an incredible gift and it can be used as a tool to bless others as well. I often find my heart is overflowing with joy once I have spent time in prayer with others and for others.

Heavenly Father, give me a passion for prayer. Guide me into a relationship with You that deepens each day. You want me to come to you about everything, whether big or small, and you care about each and every detail of my life. In Jesus name, Amen.

—Natalie

Today God is stirring my heart by...

A STAR BALLOON

"You who fear him, trust in the LORD**—he is their help and shield."**

Psalm 115:11

After lunch the other day, I decided it was time to take my seven helium star balloons down off my chair. They were starting to look droopy. I started by cutting off the ribbon attached to the chair. Next, I cut the bottom of each balloon fully expecting the balloons to drop to the ground. That was not the case. There was enough helium left in them to get to the ceiling. I tried to catch each one and flatten it out but I missed two of them.

Caleb, our 3-year-old, squealed with delight as the balloons went up. I was amazed that the balloons stayed up there since each of them had a hole at the bottom. We craned our necks while enjoying our dessert. A few minutes later, the purple one slowly came down. Caleb raced over to it and excitedly punched the balloon down. He then commented "Mom, when the teal one comes down, you need to cover your ears because I'm going to punch it again." Caleb watched the balloon very faithfully.

It stayed up there much longer than the purple one. I think that is what prompted Caleb's question.

"Mommy, can you ask Jesus?"

What would you like me to ask Him?

"Can you ask Jesus to get the balloon down?"

Sure Buddy. I can do that.

And I prayed out loud and asked Jesus to get that balloon down. It didn't come down right away. Caleb said "Didn't you pray Mommy? I thought you asked Jesus to get it down." I reminded

Caleb that God did hear our prayer and would answer when He felt like it was best.

About a minute later, the balloon started coming down.

Slowly

Slowly

Slowly

As soon as Caleb could reach it, He announced "Mommy, cover your ears!" Caleb flew over and punched hard. He had conquered that balloon. You would have thought our team won the Super Bowl as we both cheered loudly.

My heart just overflowed with gratefulness for many reasons. Caleb asked me to pray about a balloon. He knew that Jesus could help with this problem. I uttered a simple prayer to Jesus to bring a balloon down and He answered. Jesus' answer didn't come right away but it did come.

In that moment, I felt challenged. Do I turn first to Jesus for help even when it seems so simple? Or do I turn to my friends or Facebook with my problems? Do I trust that God hears my prayers? Do I truly believe that God will answer my prayers even when the answer doesn't come right away? I want to be like my son Caleb. I choose to turn to Jesus first and have no doubts that He will help me. I choose to trust His timing even when it doesn't make sense.

How about you? Do you trust God with everything, even the simple things like a star balloon on the ceiling? I hope so! God is ready to hear your prayers at any time and answer at the best time.

Heavenly Father, please help me to trust You in the little things and the big things of life. You care about everything even a star balloon. My kids are watching me LORD. Help me to model how to trust in You. Thank You for the many ways You answer my prayers. Help me to trust Your timing more. In Jesus name, Amen.

—Anastasia

Today God is stirring my heart by…

BEFORE AND AFTER

"Let us draw near to God with a sincere heart in full assurance of faith, having our hearts sprinkled to cleanse us from a guilty conscience and having our bodies washed with pure water. If we deliberately keep on sinning after we have received the knowledge of the truth, no sacrifice for sins is left."

Hebrews 10:22, 26

Let's talk about before and after. I love the HGTV shows that remodel a room and show you the jaw dropping difference between the two. I love when I'm cleaning my house and it goes from looking like someone just robbed us to being spotless. And then there are personal ones that are jaw-dropping in a different way—like some mornings when I'm shocked by my before and after while getting ready for the day. The dark circles, my ghostly pale skin-tone, the unmanageable hair, increasing wrinkles, and the stinky smell from my night of sweating. All fixed by a shower, priceless make-up, anti-wrinkle cream (that I may or may not lay hands on before applying) and about forty minutes of drying and curling my hair. And then I look at myself in the mirror and I am impressed, and yet insulted by the time and effort that went into the transformation.

We also have a spiritual transformation in Christ that takes a lot of effort and time... and each day we are able to begin again! Ephesians 4:22–24 says, "You were taught, with regard to your former way of life, to put off your old self, which is being corrupted by its deceitful desires; to be made new in the attitude of your minds; and to put on the new self, created to be like God in true righteousness and holiness." We are to throw off our old self! But I began to think, how many times do we just cover it up, like my morning routine?

When we cover up our sins and struggles we are only helping one person—Satan. Have you struggled with something, only to pour yourself into something else, hoping it will distract you from your weakness? Have you spoken unkindly about someone, hoping it would make your struggle less offensive? We try and excel in something so hopefully people don't notice our faults. Do you cover your sins/struggles up with excuses and with the phrases, "It's just the way I am," or "There are so many other sins that are worse than mine." Anyone? I can't be the only one with a raised hand. When we bring our struggles and sin to light, not only can God use them for His advantage, but we can also experience a true freedom when they are exposed and not just covered up!

Heavenly Father, You tell me in Your word to throw off everything that hinders me and run the race marked out for me. Please show me the areas where I am covering up my sins and struggles and give me the power to face them head on, making the changes that honor You! In Jesus name, Amen.

—Natalie

Today God is stirring my heart by…

ON MY KNEES

"So come, let us worship: bow before him, on your knees before GOD, who made us! Oh yes, he's our God, and we're the people he pastures, the flock he feeds.

Psalm 95:6–7, MSG

The kitchen is a mess. I went to bed way too late and woke up tired. There are texts sitting on my phone that I need to respond to. My daughter is having a complete meltdown because she doesn't have the shirt she wants to wear. My son won't put his tennis shoes on like I asked him to because he wants to wear his boots. There are a million and one things to do before I need to leave for my meeting. The stress level is rising, I snapped at my daughter, and if I don't leave now, I am going to be late!!

Do you have mornings like this? You are not alone. No really. You are not alone. We have all had these mornings more times than we can count. The question at this point is how the rest of the day is going to go. That often depends on how we react in these moments. Will we choose to give into our frustration and camp there? Or will we make the choice to put our eyes back on Jesus?

In the moments that things feel out of control, I want to get into the practice of literally getting on my knees before God. When I am in the position and humble before Him, I recognize that God has this and has never left my side. And in that moment, I can just worship instead of worry. I can be filled with joy instead of anger. The Holy Spirit living in me can help me stay self-controlled when I want to yell at my daughter or throw my sons boots out the door. God gives me wisdom to know what things I need to get done before leaving and what can wait.

When we take the focus off of our frustrations and put our eyes back where they belong on Jesus, the day really can change. So, the next time you have one of those mornings, I encourage you to get on your knees. Ask God for His help. Recognize that God has it all under control. Worship Him with singing or through prayer. Ask Him to fill you with His joy.

Heavenly Father, I need You. I can't do this parenting journey on my own. In the times where things are crazy and out of control, please help me to get on my knees before You. Please help me to recognize that You have it all under control. Thank You for caring so deeply about me. In Jesus name, Amen.

—Anastasia

Today God is stirring my heart by…

PROMISES
AND PRAISES

"I will extol the LORD at all times; his praise will always be on my lips."

Psalm 34:1

There are so many times when the evil in the world presses down and we have such hard stuff to process emotionally, mentally, and spiritually. During those moments, through deep sadness and a heavy heart, I am reminded that God will be victorious in the end, when it really matters, but it doesn't completely take away the heartache.

As I wrestle with my thoughts and prayers about the evil that surrounds us, I continually feel God responding with: Remember MY promises and praise ME. God has promised that He is faithful. God has promised a seat at His table. God has promised that He will make all things good for His purpose. God has promised never to leave us or forsake us. God has promised us life after death. God has promised hope to the hopeless. Psalm 145:13b says, "The LORD is faithful to all his promises and loving toward all he has made."

Now that we have proclaimed his promises, let's praise Him for them! "I will proclaim the name of the LORD, Oh, praise the greatness of our God." Deuteronomy 32:3

"For great is the LORD and most worthy of praise; he is to be feared above all gods." 1 Chronicles 16:25

"Naked I came from my mother's womb, and naked I will depart. The LORD gave and the LORD has taken away; may the name of the LORD be praised." Job 1:21

"I will praise you, O LORD, with all my heart; I will tell of all your wonders. I will be glad and rejoice in you; I will sing praise to your name, O Most High." Psalm 9:1–2

"Why are you downcast, O my soul? Why so disturbed within me? Put your hope in God, for I will yet praise him, my Savior and my God." Psalm 42:5

Over and over again, God's Word remains true. Praise God that He is faithful with His promises. Praise pushes away the enemy. The enemy can't be where the name of Jesus is spoken. When we sing and speak praises to God, the enemy has to flee.

Heavenly Father, great are you LORD and most worthy of my praise, for Your greatness no one can fathom (Psalm 145:3). Through Jesus, let me continually offer to you a sacrifice of praise—the fruit of my lips that confess your name. And do not let me forget to do good and to share with others, for with such sacrifices, God, You are pleased. (Hebrews 13:15) In Jesus name, Amen.

—Natalie

Today God is stirring my heart by…

SYCAMORE TREE

"When Jesus reached the spot, he looked up and said to him, "Zacchaeus, come down immediately. I must stay at your house today."

Luke 19:

The story of Zacchaeus has always been one that intrigues me. It's only ten verses long but so much is packed into his story. I have lots to learn from this wee little man. He was determined, a good listener, repentant, and one who acted on his word.

Zacchaeus was a man of great wealth. He didn't lack anything. But, yet he lacked the most important thing—life with Jesus as his Savior and LORD. One day Jesus was passing through Jericho. Zacchaeus heard about Jesus but wanted to see who He was. But because he was short, he couldn't see over the crowd. Zacchaeus was determined though. He ran ahead and climbed a sycamore tree just to see Jesus. I am challenged by this. Do I run ahead and climb so I can see Jesus? Do I let go of my distractions and do what it takes to see Jesus?

The story continues with Zacchaeus waiting in the tree to get a glimpse of Jesus. When Jesus passed by the spot, He looked up at Zacchaeus and asked him to come done immediately. Zacchaeus was a good listener at this point. He could of said "Am I really worthy to spend time with?" or "Are you sure you're talking to the right man?" Instead of responding in that way, he listened. Zacchaeus came right down and welcomed Jesus. When Jesus asks me to come down from my pride, my doubts, my worries, my fears, my judgmental attitude, do I respond like Zacchaeus? Do I climb down right away and welcome Jesus? Or do I give excuses for my sin?

After Zacchaeus welcomed Jesus into his home, he also welcomed Him into his heart. He admitted to doing wrong to people. Zacchaeus was repentant. Not only was he repentant, he acted. He realized how much he cheated people. Instead of just paying back the amount he cheated them, he decided to pay back four times the amount. In addition to that, Zacchaeus also gave half of what he owned to the poor. This my friends is a result of changed heart. He listened to Jesus and responded. Once again, I am challenged by this man. Do I respond to the conviction of the Holy Spirit when I sin? Am I repentant? What changes do I make in my life in response to what God is teaching me?

Zacchaeus may have been a short man, but he was a smart man. One climb up a sycamore tree changed his life forever. He opened his heart to Jesus and was never the same. My prayer is that I learn from this wee little man. I want to do what it takes to see Jesus—run, climb, etc. I also want to be one who listens to Jesus and becomes more in tune with His voice. But not only that, I want to respond to what Jesus is asking me to do. I want to be a different person each time I encounter my Jesus.

How about you? Will you do what it takes to meet Jesus? To listen and change to be more like Him? My friend, you will be beyond blessed if you do. Learn from Zacchaeus today.

Heavenly Father, thank You for the story of Zacchaeus. God, I want to do whatever it takes to see You. I want to listen to You and be more in tune with Your voice. Holy Spirit, please help me to respond to what you are teaching me and change as needed. Thank You for your patience with me. I love You, LORD. In Jesus name, Amen.

—Anastasia

Today God is stirring my heart by…

JUMP FROM
THE TOP STEP

*"Trust in the LORD with all your heart and lean not on
your own understanding; in all your ways acknowledge
him, and he will make your paths straight."*

Proverbs 3: 5–6

I love the moments when you step back and watch a child teach you something. One day at my in-laws, my sweet, spunky niece did just that. In their last house there was a short flight of stairs and all the grandkids loved to stand at the very top and jump into your arms at the bottom. What really grabbed my attention was how my niece was doing it. She had absolute—100% trust in my husband as he caught her. She was not scared to jump, she did it with force. She was not timid, in fact, she threw her arms, head and legs back and even closed her eyes… free as a bird!

It made me think about what our faith looks like to God in our situations. Do we plunge whole heart and completely zealous into trusting God? Or do we cower, turn away, or walk a few steps down and then jump? Do we trust as long as we can keep hold of a little control? The story of David and Goliath comes to my mind and how the situations in our lives feel like a giant against us. Not only did David volunteer to fight the Philistine, but King Saul tried to put Armor on him to help protect him, but he refused. He knew God would protect him, and with God's help he would defeat the enemy.

How often do we put our trust into something so that we have a safety net? People, worldly possessions, job, money, ourselves…the list could go on. It's hard to trust in God's direction, His timing, His reasons at times, but God promises not to leave or forsake us. When we are fully able to trust God, a sense of peace will wash over us. It says in Isaiah 26:3–4, "You will keep in perfect peace him whose mind is steadfast, because he trusts in you. Trust in the LORD forever, for the LORD, the LORD, is the Rock eternal."

We can never avoid hardships, making decisions, or the downfall of man, but we always have a God that we can turn to and put all our trust in! Are you allowing God to be your rock today?

Heavenly Father, thank You that no matter what is going on in my life, You are my rock and I know that I can trust in You at all times. In Jesus name, Amen.

—Natalie

Today God is stirring my heart by…

MOMENTS
THAT MATTER

"Let your eyes look straight ahead; fix your gaze directly before you."

Proverbs 4:25

I have been on a hunt lately. It's a hunt I plan to be on the rest of my life. This hunt is not easy, sometimes it's downright hard, but I know it's totally worth it. I am on a hunt for Moments That Matter.

What is a moment that matters? It is something that happens with your spouse, your child, a friend, or a loved one. A moment where you just want to memorize and hold on to. These moments have been happening for a while now, but until the past couple months I haven't slowed down enough to see them. I mean REALLY see the moments.

My journey began in May of 2014. I started reading a book called "Hands Free Mama" by Rachel Macy Stafford. It has changed my life and the life of my family. I read through about half the book and started to implement what I learned right away. I realized several things while reading this book. One was that I was entirely too distracted by my phone. Email, text, and Facebook took a lot of my time. I was noticing that I was so distracted from being a wife and mom because I spent so much of my time on the phone. I would be very annoyed when the kids interrupted me. God got a hold of my heart as I read this book and reminded me of what I was home full time for. He also helped me to see how I was letting my 'to do' list define my day instead of the Moments that Matter.

I am so thankful for the changes I have implemented. I was very determined at first and did really well with being on my phone at certain times. After a month or two, I could tell a shift in my attitude and my kids. I took a hard look at how I was using my time and realized I was on my phone at times where I needed to focus on my kids. I needed to implement once again what I had learned. I actually finished the book and reviewed all I had learned. It was so helpful and I got back on track. I started the hunt once again for the Moments that Matter. There are two stories that have happened recently that I am so thankful I didn't miss.

One Wednesday morning, I had a chiropractic appointment. While waiting to be called back, this is one of those times that I try to play with the kids and just be with them. Well, that particular morning we had a friend along and the girls were playing really well. My son Caleb was lounging and reading.

So, I pulled out my phone to catch up on texts. I mean, why not, right? Any Mom understands the need to take a breather especially when all is quiet. Soon after pulling out my phone, Caleb tried to climb up in my lap with a book. In that moment I had a choice. I could choose to put down my phone and read to Caleb. Or I could try to get him to entertain himself once again. I'll be totally honest, I hesitated. But, then I put my phone down, and pulled him into my lap.

What ended up happening next was precious. Caleb, who was 2 years old at that time, started pointing at all the different pictures in the book and reciting the names—apples, bunny, train, balloons, etc. He exploded with vocabulary that I hadn't heard from him before. Caleb "read" the book to me many times before I was called back for my appointment. It was a Moment That Mattered. I'm so glad I didn't miss it.

A few days later I was able to have another Moment That Mattered. My kids walk down about a block and a half to get to the bus stop. It's a little hard to see them as they walk, but my goal is to be present. I love to communicate to them they are worth my time. This is one of those times where it is very easy for me to glance at my phone. To check email, text or that Facebook notification that came across. That morning I thought to myself, "Well, my kids can't see me anyway so I might as well check my phone." But, I remembered my journey and stopped myself from pulling it out. I could see that the kids made it to the stop.

And in that moment, as I looked down at the bus stop, Micaela, my daughter lifted her neon yellow gloved hand and waved big. This Mom saw that hand and waved big right back. To think, I could have missed that precious moment. That was a moment that mattered.

As I stated earlier, this journey is not easy. Sometimes it's downright hard. I have to break the patterns of being on my phone too much that have been there for awhile. It's easy to fall back into it. But, I won't stop this journey. I'll keep looking for those Moments that Matter. I don't want to miss them!

Heavenly Father, thank You for all that You have been teaching me about moments that matter. I want to continue to be on the hunt for these moments. Holy Spirit, please prompt and remind me to be present when I am with my loved ones. Thank You. In Jesus name, Amen.

—Anastasia

Today God is stirring my heart by…

YOUR
BEST YES

"It is not good to have zeal without knowledge, nor to be hasty and miss the way."

Proverbs 19:2

I have no idea how to juggle objects. I've tried many times, people have tried to teach me, and I just can't get it. I either drop something, or an object hits me in the head, and then I finally just throw everything up in the air and run away. The people that can juggle knives, chainsaws, or flaming sticks seriously blow my mind and they have my total and utter respect. However, as a mom I do juggle many things, as I'm sure you do also. All week long I'm striving to keep these all going, hoping none will fall. And yet, I'm so quick to add more, which leads to a more hectic schedule, which leads to my priorities changing, which leads to more stress, and usually ends with me feeling like I have failed everything. Or I feel like throwing everything up in the air and running away! Can you relate?

God tells us it's good to have zeal, but not without knowledge. I think as believers we feel that if it is something good, that we are supposed to do it—which isn't always true. It says in Romans 12:11, "Never be lacking in zeal, but keep your spiritual fervor, serving the LORD." I think an even simpler way to say this is—never lose your zeal, but keep it focused on God. Just because something is "good," doesn't mean it is wise for you to do it.

Too often we can spread ourselves so thin on things that God maybe isn't even calling us to do. We need to be more diligent at asking God first which things we need to juggle! How different would our lives look if we backed our zeal with the things God wants us to pour into? What would your life look like if you stopped and asked God first what He wants you to do? Are there things in your life that you need to give up so that you can fill it with the things God is asking of you?

Heavenly Father, You have given me many talents and gifts, but if I am not using them on things that You have called me to do, then I'm not using them for Your glory. Show me how to identify the things that are good, but maybe not beneficial to me or Your Kingdom. Help me to keep my zeal on the things You have called of me. In Jesus name, Amen.

—Natalie

Today God is stirring my heart by…

LIFE SONG

"He will rejoice over you with singing."

Zephaniah 3:17

Here I am to Worship
More Than Enough
Mighty to Save
Always

Are you familiar with these worship songs? My husband and I have them mostly memorized especially the chorus of each. Why is that? Because they are our children's life songs. What is a life song?

It all began when we decided it was time to expand our family. I devoured so many books and articles on parenting at that time. One article I read spurred on the idea to pick a life song for our children. When we found out I was pregnant with our firstborn, my husband and I began to daily pray for health for the baby and their salvation.

I also began praying and asking God what the life song of the baby was. I remember several songs coming to mind as I prayed. What song will represent this baby's life? What song will speak truth over this baby's life in the years to come? God soon clarified which one it would be for our firstborn. So, each evening when we laid hands on my belly, we would pray for the baby and then sing the baby's life song. We did this for each of our pregnancies. I loved praying and waiting for God to show me what the life song would be for each of our children.

To this day, we sing each of our children's life songs after we pray for them in the evenings. The kids know each other's songs and will even sing along sometimes. In fact, often when we are out doing errands and listening to the radio, we will hear one of the kid's life songs. I love watching the kids come alive, take ownership and loudly sing their life song. My husband and I even had a life song picked out for the baby we miscarried in between our two older children. Jeremiah's song brings me great comfort any time I hear it. And I love that when our other kids hear "Everlasting God" they remember their brother too. I'm excited to see how our children live out the message of their life song in the years to come.

The other day, one of my children asked me what my life song was. I loved that they assumed everyone has a life song. I explained that I didn't have one because it wasn't something my parents did. That conversation has got me thinking though. What is my life song? It's not too late for me to pray for that song. I'm going to start praying about it and see what my Heavenly Daddy gives me for a life song.

How about you? What is your life song? I am sure God has one for you. Pray about it. If you're pregnant, I encourage you to pray about a life song for your baby. And even if your children are older you can still pray about a life song for their life.

Heavenly Father, I am amazed that You sing over me. It must be a very beautiful song. Thank You for loving me and speaking truth over me. Help me to live out Your will for my life. I desire to bless You and worship You with all that I am. I love You, LORD. In Jesus name, Amen.

—Anastasia

Today God is stirring my heart by…

MY HOLY SPIRIT

"The tongue has the power of life and death, and those who love it will eat its fruit."

Proverbs 18:21

A couple years ago I had a one-of-a-kind experience. My husband and I, along with some friends from church, filmed a reality TV show episode. Yes, you read that correctly. It still feels a little surreal even to write about it. During that time, God had pressed upon my heart to be aware of the words I speak. For three days I had a microphone strapped to me—we referred to it as "My Holy Spirit." Oh how true. Shouldn't we all walk around with a constant reminder to be watchful of our words! Let me tell you, after being a stay-at-home mom for a decade, it had been years since I felt this submerged in "the world" being with Hollywood crew and producers, trying to speak truth and life while all along they are trying to make the opposite happen. What a challenge and eye-opening experience!

So take a minute and think about the people around you, your circumstances and your opportunities that can be affected by your words. Those hurting and in need a word of encouragement— "Pleasant words are a honeycomb, sweet to the soul and healing to the bones." Proverbs 16:24. Or someone that needs to hear something God has placed on your heart—"A word aptly spoken is like apples of gold in settings of silver." Proverbs 25:11. Maybe there is someone that needs or deserves your praise—"Let another praise you, and not your own mouth; someone else, and not your own lips." Proverbs 27:2.

Then I think about the times my words have caused damage— "Reckless words pierce like a sword, but the tongue of the wise brings healing." Proverbs 12:18. Or when I am upset about something or someone, or maybe when I'm sitting around chatting with friends and let my words carelessly come out—"When words are many, sin is not absent, but he who holds his tongue is wise." Proverbs 10:19.

What a great reminder that we have the power of life and death! How are you using your words today? Join me today and let's strap the Holy Spirit to us as we use our words to bring life around us!

Heavenly Father, You tell us in Your word that the lips of the righteous know what is fitting—help me LORD to stay in tune with Your Spirit so that I can acknowledge that very thing. Bring me so close to You that I know immediately what words to use and the words to hold back. In Jesus name, Amen.

—Natalie

Today God is stirring my heart by…

SIT AT THE FEET
Part 1

"Her sister, Mary, sat at the LORD's feet, listening to what he taught. But Martha was distracted by the big dinner she was preparing. She came to Jesus and said, "LORD, doesn't it seem unfair to you that my sister just sits here while I do all the work? Tell her to come and help me." But the LORD said to her, "My dear Martha, you are worried and upset over all these details! There is only one thing worth being concerned about. Mary has discovered it, and it will not be taken away from her."

Luke 10:39–42

You are flying around the house with the last minute clean up. Or maybe you haven't even started clean up. So, you are shoving things in the closets, wiping toothpaste out of the sink, and yelling to your son to put his shoes away. Your guests are going to be here very soon. Oh and dinner, that's right! It's time to get the casserole in the oven so it's done on time. Do you feel your heart racing just reading this? Are you reminded of times this has happened to you?

In our key verses for today, we are jumping into a story of two women. We will take two days to look at this story since there is so much packed into it. Jesus has arrived at the house of Mary and Martha. He is there to visit and teach.

Martha is the housekeeper and hard at work. We can learn a lot from Martha in this story. Martha has a great work ethic. She also has the gift of hospitality. A downside of this gift is that Martha was distracted by her work. Her distractions lead to whining and complaining. What can we learn from Martha?

First, let's look at how focused Martha is. Honestly, I admire Martha's work ethic. I also admire her hospitality. Jesus stopped by unannounced yet she welcomed Him into her home. She set right to work to get food ready for her guests. You have to remember that this wasn't a few friends that stopped by. Probably more like a small crowd. Jesus most likely came with all twelve disciples. There were several others that followed Jesus that also probably came into the home.

I love how hard Martha worked. There is nothing wrong with being a hard worker. In fact, we read in Colossians 3:23 "Whatever you do, work at it with all your heart, as working for the LORD, not for human masters." God wants us to be hard workers. What He doesn't want is for us to be so distracted by our work that we don't take time to be with Him. Martha needed to not let her work distract her from being with Jesus.

God also desires us to have self-control when we feel overwhelmed. Martha had a lot happening to get ready for her guests. She started to get really upset with her sister Mary. Martha even went as far as to complain and whine to Jesus about it. In the moments we feel overwhelmed, we need to take a step back, breathe and ask Jesus to help us be self-controlled. We also need to ask Him to help us not point to others and blame them for feeling the way we do. It wasn't Mary's fault that Martha was stressed. Martha made the choice to be distracted.

I love how Jesus lovingly confronts this choice in Luke 10:41–42 "But the LORD said to her, "My dear Martha, you are worried and upset over all these details! There is only one thing worth being concerned about. Mary has discovered it, and it will not be taken away from her." Jesus reminds Martha that the only thing worth being concerned about is taking time to be with Jesus. This is something that can never be taken away. Jesus wanted Martha to see how much her work was taking away from learning more about Him. He wanted her to realize the importance of spending time at His feet every day. Jesus also wanted Martha to see that she could talk to Him at any time.

How do we apply this to our lives? I think it's safe to say that as women we are always working on something. We have lists galore and things around the house and work that needs to get done. Jesus loves that we work hard. What Jesus loves even more than that is when we take time to be with Him and just Jesus. In tomorrow's devotional we will take a look at how Mary made the choice to sit at the feet.

Heavenly Father, thank You for affirming my hard work. There are so many details to keep up with each day and many things to do. Thank You that You care about it all and want to help me. God, I long to not let my work distract me from You. Holy Spirit, please prompt me when I get too overwhelmed. Please help me to pause and slow down. Please help me to hold my tongue and take full responsibility for my actions. Jesus, I want You first in my life and in my heart. Please guide me in how to do this. I love You, LORD. In Jesus name, Amen.

—Anastasia

Today God is stirring my heart by…

SIT AT THE FEET
Part 2

"Her sister, Mary, sat at the LORD's feet, listening to what he taught. But Martha was distracted by the big dinner she was preparing. She came to Jesus and said, "LORD, doesn't it seem unfair to you that my sister just sits here while I do all the work? Tell her to come and help me." But the LORD said to her, "My dear Martha, you are worried and upset over all these details! There is only one thing worth being concerned about. Mary has discovered it, and it will not be taken away from her."

Luke 10:39–42

Think about the last time you sat down. Did you have a child in your lap? Maybe you were you talking to a friend or texting someone. Were you paying the bills or catching up on email? We can get a lot done when we sit down. In today's key verses, we read about what Mary did when she sat down.

Jesus had just stopped by for a visit. While her sister Martha was rushing around getting things ready, Mary made a different choice that day. She humbled herself and she opened her heart.

Mary made the choice to slow down. There were many things around the house to get done but Mary was concerned about the only thing worth being concerned about. She decided to not let the things of the world dictate what she should be doing. Mary chose to sit down.

Mary also humbled herself. Did you notice where Mary sat? At the feet of Jesus. This is a very humbling position. Mary declared that Jesus was her LORD and savior. She made the statement to all around her that she was going to submit to Jesus.

Mary also opened her heart. As she sat at Jesus' feet she chose to listen. Mary wanted to be more like Jesus so as He spoke, she soaked in each word. I believe that as Mary listened she was looking deep into her own heart to see what she needed to change.

Like Mary, we have a choice each day. Will we let the long to do lists, the project due at work, or even our own kids distract us from the choice to be with Jesus? We need to make time to be with Jesus daily. Time at His feet. We will be blessed by taking this time. Not only will God overflow us with His peace and joy but we will learn how to be more like Jesus. When we open our hearts to Him and ask Jesus to change us, God always comes through. Will you join me in sitting at the feet of Jesus every day?

Heavenly Father, this week was crazy. Almost too busy. As I look back now, I realize even more of my need to slow down. Jesus, I want to make it a priority to sit at Your feet and just listen. Please teach me to humble myself before You. I want to let go off all the distractions and focus on You alone Jesus. In Jesus name, Amen.

—Anastasia

Today God is stirring my heart by…

WHERE DO YOU FIND YOUR WORTH?

"When the LORD saw that Leah was not loved, he opened her womb, but Rachel was barren. Leah became pregnant and gave birth to a son. She named him Reuben, for she said, "It is because the LORD has seen my misery. Surely my husband will love me now.

Genesis 29: 31–32

Lately I've been reading about Jacob, Rachel, and Leah and I think my jaw has dropped quite a few times. I've read their story before, but never really grasped the amount of sin, jealousy, revenge, deceit, pride, and unacceptance it held. And as you continue reading how it affected all the brothers and ensued generations of hatred. There is so much to learn from their situation, so I will be splitting it up and covering different topics over the next couple days. Today, we are going to talk about Leah.

My heart went out to Leah. I'm a huge sports fan and if I'm watching a game that my team isn't playing in, I always cheer for the underdog. When reading this scripture, that's what Leah felt like to me—the underdog of this story. How hurtful for her to experience not being wanted or chosen; and it wasn't even her doing. Her father gave her away to Jacob. A man that didn't want her, a man that wanted her sister and made sure everyone knew it.

Leah begged God to give her a child in hopes it would help Jacob fall in love with her. Heartbreaking, isn't? Have you ever felt unwanted? I have. It's not a good feeling. When I look at Leah and examine her life, I can't help but notice that she looked to others for her self-worth and favor on her life. But God tells us in Proverbs 8:35, "For whoever finds me finds life and receives favor from the LORD." Makes me pause and examine my life a bit. Where am I finding my worth? In my husband, kids, writing success, my home, who my friends are, what strengths I have to offer? How about you?

Let's backtrack a bit in Proverbs to 8:17–21, "I love those who love me, and those who seek me find me. With me are riches and honor, enduring wealth and prosperity. My fruit is better than fine gold; what I yield surpasses choice silver. I walk in the way of righteousness, along the paths of justice, bestowing wealth on those who love me and making their treasuries full." A couple things I took from these verses…

First, Leah thought she needed a son to have worth and be accepted (notice she kept having children, but it never filled that gap, that longing to be accepted). But in God we find our riches, worth, and prosperity. God doesn't love us because we have or haven't done something. He simply loves us because we are His.

Second, God says that His fruit is better than fine gold. What God pours into us will always be enough. Always. We should never have to look beyond God to others or "positions" to fill any holes— God wants to make our treasuries full with the love of Him alone. The great thing about being a follower of Christ is that we are always wanted by the King. We never have to wonder. So on days when my heart is hurt and I try to grasp onto other things for my worth, I can rest in the joy that I am wanted and loved, and in God I find where I belong!

Heavenly Father, You have created my inmost being; You knit me together in my mother's womb. I praise You because I am fearfully and wonderfully made; Your works are wonderful, I know that full well (Psalm 139: 13–14). In Jesus name, Amen.

—Natalie

Today God is stirring my heart by...

THE GREEN-
EYED MONSTER

"When Rachel saw that she was not bearing Jacob any children, she became jealous of her sister. So she said to Jacob, "Give me children, or I'll die!" Jacob became angry with her and said, "Am I in the place of God, who has kept you from having children?" Then she said, "Here is Bilhah, my maidservant. Sleep with her so that she can bear children for me and that through her I too can build a family."

Genesis 30:1–3

When reading this passage and taking a good look at Rachel, one word sticks out to me. Jealousy. Rachel became so jealous of her sister Leah because she could give Jacob children while she remained barren. So jealous in fact, that she took matters into her own hands and had her maidservant sleep with him so she could have children through her. And it didn't stop there. It actually got worse. Then Leah couldn't conceive, so she had Jacob sleep with her maidservant. And for years this went back and forth between them. Finally the LORD heard Rachel's cry and she gave birth to Joseph. Joseph then became Jacob's favorite and his brothers became extremely jealous of him. So jealous, that the brothers ended up selling him into slavery—but that's a story for another day.

Let's take a look at a couple scriptures that tells us about jealousy. In 2 Corinthians 12:20 we have Paul sharing his concerns to the Corinthians. "For I am afraid that when I come I may not find you as I want you to be, and you may not find me as you want me to be. I fear that there may be quarreling, jealousy, outburst of anger, factions, slander, gossip, arrogance and disorder." Did you notice in that list you usually have jealousy with at least one of the others?

Now flip over to Galatians 5:19–20, "The acts of the sinful nature are obvious; sexual immorality, impurity and debauchery; idolatry and witchcraft; hatred, discord, jealousy, fits of rage, selfish ambition, dissensions, and factions." Hmmm, are you seeing a theme here? I am. God compiles jealousy with some pretty ugly sins. It also makes me think about how ugly my heart looks to God when I store jealousy in it. The thing with jealousy is that it never just stays in our heart, it leaks out and causes destruction around us, a bitter wake from our path, and another stepping stone to more sins. It alters our actions, words, and perspective.

Let's take a serious look at jealousy and how it can corrupt us. Often times when we compare ourselves to others, it births a seed of jealously that quickly grows. We become jealous over how people look, their positions, someone has what we want, the loss of another's affection/time, others getting the blessings when we feel like we only get the leftovers—the list could go on. Often times when we harbor jealousy in our hearts, we can't see what God has right in front of us. Rachel let her jealousy ruin her relationship with her sister. Rachel let her jealousy become self-destructive and consume her. Rachel had a husband that loved her deeply, despite whether she could conceive or not, and she dismissed that devotion for her own selfish desires.

Take a moment to pause and reflect on your life. How are you struggling with jealousy? We all do—we just have to find the source and look to Christ for the freedom over it.

Heavenly Father, as water reflects a face, so a man's heart reflects the man. LORD, I do not want my heart to reflect jealousy. Please help me to identify those areas that I struggle in this and help me break free. In Jesus name, Amen.

—Natalie

Today God is stirring my heart by...

BE AN EXAMPLE

"Now Israel (Jacob) loved Joseph more than any of his other sons, because he had been born to him in his old age; and he made a richly ornamented robe for him. When his brothers saw that their father loved him more than any of them, they hated him and could not speak a kind word to him."

Genesis 37: 3–4

You know that person that gets under your skin. That rubs you raw. Makes your blood pressure spike and you wonder, "Am I going to have a stroke?" Yep, that's the one. Well, I have one. Two, sometimes. Alright, let's just say three... ahem, moving on! There have been times I've wanted to revert back to Bible times and have uproar like Jesus did in the temple. I would have loved to throw a few tables myself. Clearly Jesus had the right, and with good reason... mine would have been just because I was upset or hurt. So instead of throwing tables, I threw a few frustrated words that oh so easily spilled out from my not so holy mouth. I held a grudge. I struggled to forgive.

Recalling those times, I began to wonder how Jesus would react. What He would say? What advice would He give? Then my thoughts trickled to, why are these people in my life? God's quiet spirit reminded me that as I go through training and disciplining my children, He is also doing that for me through those individuals. He is molding and teaching me. He is showing me the righteous way to respond, instead of the sinful one that comes effortlessly. Teaching me that instead of broadcasting all their faults, pray for these people, because it's not my job to fix them, it's His.

We, as moms, have a great responsibility to model how to deal with these people in our lives. When we read about Jacob's sons we see so much anger, resentment, and jealousy. Hmmm, does that sound familiar? Isn't that exactly what Jacob, Rachel and Leah went through? Instead of showing their children the righteous way to respond, they displayed the sinful one that led to sad and bitter consequences among all the children, and how that hatred grew so much they ended up selling Joseph into slavery.

I had to stop and ask myself: What example are you giving your children? What words are they overhearing you say? Ouch. In 1 John 2: 10–11 it says, "Whoever loves his brother lives in the light, and there is nothing in him to make him stumble. But whoever hates his brother is in the darkness and walks around in the darkness; he does not know where he is going, because the darkness has blinded him." Does this mean we are to like everyone? No. But it's about our attitude. It's how we handle these people and the situations that arise around them and to love them through Christ.

My son handed me a piece of humble pie a couple years ago. Jarrett came home so upset because a boy in his class had been so mean to him. In fact, he cried for an hour that night in bed. The next week was his birthday party at school and I made cupcakes with each of the students' names on them. In my dislike over this child that had hurt my son's feelings, I put his name on the worst and smallest cupcake. Yep, I am admitting that I was deliberately mean to a seven-year-old. Not my finest moment! At the party, they played a game and Jarrett could pick someone to come up front with him (huge honor to a 2nd grader to be picked). You want to know who he picked? He chose the kid that had been so mean to him. In my darkness of wanting to stick it to this kid and give him the worst cupcake, it had blinded me to loving on this kid instead. Maybe he needed a word of encouragement or just a smile or maybe the biggest and best cupcake I made.

We can never control how people will react, what people will say, what people will do—but we can always control the way we react, the words we say and what we do!! Do you have an opportunity to bring healing to a relationship? Forgiveness? Let God work through you so you are able to walk in the light and not be blinded by the darkness.

Heavenly Father, You know the people in my life that cause strife in my heart. As I go through training and disciplining my children, do the same for me through these individuals. Mold me to speak only kindness, work on my heart to forgive—even if it's not asked for or deserved. Guide me to pray for these people and love on them through You and with Your strength. In Jesus name, Amen.

—Natalie

Today God is stirring my heart by...

I WILL SCREAM!

"Like a city whose walls are broken through is a person who lacks self-control."

Proverbs 25:28

"If you blow out both the candles, I will scream!!" yelled Analiah to her brother Caleb. We were at lunch one day with candles lit. At the end of the meal, the kids were each allowed to blow out one candle. Caleb went first and looked like he was going to blow out both. Analiah did not want that to happen so she very sternly told Caleb what not to do. And Analiah also clearly told Caleb what she would do if he blew out her candle.

It was in the moment that I intervened so World War 3 wouldn't break out. I calmly asked Analiah what she could do instead of screaming. She reviewed our standard routine when facing a challenge with a sibling. First, the kids need to talk nicely and ask the sibling to stop doing what is bothering them. If the sibling doesn't respond or stop, our kids have been instructed to ask for help. I politely asked, "Have you done this Analiah?" She replied with a "No" and then proceeded to talk politely to Caleb. Thankfully Caleb responded to her and didn't blow out the candle.

Next, the kids blew out their candles and lunch was over. As I cleaned up, the Holy Spirit stirred in my heart; "You should really follow your own advice." I felt convicted and challenged. All too often, I do feel like screaming when one of the kids talks back to me or doesn't follow through on what I have asked them to do. I need to pause and take a deep breath before I respond. I need to lead well like I often tell my kids. If they see me reacting without self-control what are they going to learn? I want to model what self-control is.

In our key verse for today, it communicates that a person who doesn't have self-control is like a city whose walls are broken through. What does that really mean? When the city walls are broken through, the city is defenseless and disgraced. Do you really want to be a person who is defenseless and disgraced? Me neither. Another verse in Proverbs 16:32 speaks about self-control: "Better a patient person than a warrior, one with self-control than one who takes a city." When you have self-control, you display great character. You may not be the warrior who takes the city but you accomplish much better things by developing the character God desires. In Galatians 5:32, one of the fruit of the Spirit is self-control. Throughout the Bible we find more verses about the importance of self-control.

God thinks self-control is pretty important. I want to be a person known for my self-control and patience. I want my kids to see me as someone who displays God's character. How about you? Are you a person who displays self-control? Do you teach your kids to have self-control? I love that God doesn't leave us hanging on this one. He has given us the Holy Spirit to guide us and help us control our tongues.

Heavenly Father, thank You for the gift of Your Holy Spirit. Thank You that You are with me to help me hold my tongue. God, I want to reflect Your character to my kids. I want to display self-control. Please help me to lead my children well. I love You, LORD. In Jesus name, Amen.
—Anastasia

Today God is stirring my heart by…

SOMETHING BETTER

"For I know the plans I have for you," declares the LORD, "plans to prosper you and not to harm you, plans to give you hope and a future."

Jeremiah 29:11

Do you ever plan to go somewhere because it will be the perfect place for your event? And then you get there and end up having to change plans after a while? This happened to my husband and I the other day. Through our experience, I learned even more about how God cares about every detail.

Jonathan and I dropped the kids off at a friend's house for most of the day. We were very excited to get our Vision Retreat started. We decided to go to a quiet place in town that was a perfect setting for a retreat. There are several nooks and comfortable areas throughout this place. We settled in the comfortable chairs by the gas fireplace. We felt relaxed and ready to hear from God.

After an hour or so of reflecting, talking and starting to plan we took a little break. After coming back, we noticed the employees starting to set up tables and chairs. They mentioned that a Christmas party was going to be held there. It wasn't going to be for another hour, so we were okay to keep working there.

Well, I am one who has a very hard time focusing when there is a lot of noise. So after about 5 minutes, we decided to move to another part of this place. It helped to get away from the noise of set up, but that area was also distracting. The speaker to their radio was booming with music. It was just too much for me so we left. I felt so frustrated. Here we are trying so hard to be focused and intentional and we kept getting interrupted.

We loaded all our things into the van and headed to a bookstore in town. The last time we had come to this bookstore it was not very quiet so I was concerned. After arriving, I was thrilled to learn the bookstore had opened up an area in their basement with tables and couches. We headed downstairs to try it out. The place was perfect. It was very quiet and much brighter than the last place we had been. My husband commented "Isn't it a blessing that we got disrupted? It pushed us in to a much better place." I wholeheartedly agreed and thanked God for the disruption that lead us to this bookstore.

God does this again and again in our lives, doesn't He? We have this great plan in mind and it seems like it's a perfect. But then something disrupts it. We question God and wonder why? We don't trust His plan for us. The truth is found in our key verse for today. God has great plans for us. They are plans that will prosper us and not harm us. Plans that give us a hope and a future. So, the next time plans change, ask God to show you how He is working in that change. Trust God that He knows best. Rest in His promise.

Heavenly Father, thank You for having great plans for me. Thank You that Your plans are not to harm me but instead to prosper me. Please help me to trust You even when things don't make sense. And when plans change, help me to see how You are working in the change. You know what is best for me. Thank You for loving me. In Jesus name, Amen.

—Anastasia

Today God is stirring my heart by…

NOT A BURDEN, BUT A JOY

"Whatever you do, work at it with all your heart, as working for the LORD, not for men."

Colossians 3:23

Lately I have been reminded over and over of how important our position of a mom is and it renewed my passion to be better. First, God has entrusted us to care for His children. He chose you specifically, without a doubt, to be the mother of your children. Second, we are to take this blessing of being a mom and not just survive, but thrive!

One night I was reading to my boys their Bible story before bed and we were talking about the Israelites and how they were slaves before God used Moses to rescue and save them. My son stopped me and asked me, "What is a slave?" I replied, "Well, it's someone that has to work for someone else without pay or appreciation. Their life is totally dedicated to serving someone." And then I laughed. I think that might be the definition of "Mother" on Google.

How easy can our role as wife and/or mother be related to a slave. And let me tell you, that's where we can get into trouble, when we look at our work as a task, and not an act of worship. That is how I can often feel about unending laundry, dishes, urine sprayed bathrooms, meals, cleaning, picking up after three kids that feel like eight... all consuming! But I am not a slave to my "to do" list. Oh no, I am a follower of Christ that has the great opportunity to worship my King by serving those around me!

God tells us in 1 Peter 4:11, "If anyone speaks, he should do it as one speaking the very words of God. If anyone serves, he should do it with the strength God provides, so that in all things God may be praised through Jesus Christ. To him be the glory and the power for ever and ever. Amen." We were never meant to do this on our own, so why do we often try? What better example can we be for our children than to show that when we serve we are doing it by the strength God provides. And how would our family feel if they knew it wasn't a burden to serve them, but a joy.

Heavenly Father, thank You for granting me the blessing of being a mom. What an amazing gift to raise children and teach them about You. Help me to keep the perspective that I'm doing this for You. What an honor to raise Your children that You have entrusted to me. In Jesus name, Amen.

—Natalie

Today God is stirring my heart by…

THE FIRST
TO LET GO

"Slow down. Take a deep breath. What's the hurry?"

Jeremiah 2:25a, MSG

Hugging. When you read that word you may cringe or you might smile. Depending on how you grew up can often determine whether you like hugs or not. I was not raised in a family that hugged a much. After I was married, hugging needed to become a priority since it is my husband's top love language. Since becoming a Mom, I have learned the importance of giving your kids a hug. It communicates so much to them. The other day, I learned another lesson about hugs.

When it comes to hugs, I don't ever want to be the first to let go. I am trying to live this motto out with my kids. The other day, I went into my son Caleb's room to get him up for the day. After pulling him out of his crib, he threw his arms around me and snuggled for a hug. It was a Moment That Mattered. Caleb held on tight and I hugged him right back. As I stood there, my mind starting racing about all the things that needed to get done that day. I was just about to put Caleb down so we could get going on our day. In that moment, God whispered to my heart. "Don't be the first to let go. Spend this precious time with Caleb." When I continued to hug Caleb in that moment, I communicated to him that he was more important that what I had going and what I wanted to get done.

I am so thankful I listened to God's voice in that moment. As soon as Caleb did let go, he was off and running. To think what I could have missed that moment. It made me more aware for the rest of the day. Later that morning, he hugged me again and I had to remind myself to not be the first to let go. These are the moments that are precious. These are the moments that matter. My 'to do' list will always be there but these moments with my children will not. I want to take advantage of these moments as much as I can. Like our key verse states, I want to learn to slow down and take a deep breath. I don't always want to be in a hurry.

Here's a challenge for you: the next time your child≠ or even your husband gives you a hug, don't be the first one to let go. Communicate to them in that hug that they are more important than what you had going or even what you want to get done. Pause and embrace that moment. Let them be the first to let go.

Heavenly Father, please teach me how to slow down and take a deep breath. I long to communicate to my husband and children how much they mean to me. I want to take time to hug and hold them until they let go first. Holy Spirit, please prompt me to embrace these moments with my family. Thank You for helping me. In Jesus name, Amen.

—Anastasia

Today God is stirring my heart by…

_____

_____

_____

_____

_____

_____

_____

_____

_____

_____

GUARD YOUR HEART

"Be wise in the way you act toward outsiders; make the most of every opportunity. Let your conversation be always full of grace, seasoned with salt, so that you may know how to answer everyone."

Colossians 4:5–6

I know this scripture is meant to focus on our interactions with unbelievers, but why not take it one step forward and replace outsiders with others. At all times, whether we are with an unbeliever, a believer, family, friends, co-workers (the list could go on), we are to represent these verses. When I read these words I couldn't get past the "make the most of every opportunity." It reminded that God puts opportunities in our path and if we are not prepared or walking in His way, we *will* miss what He has set up.

I felt like I biffed it big time on my first book signing. I prayed before I went, but most of it concerned my nervousness. During the hours I sat there a cleaning lady came past and looked at my book, asking questions. She sat it down and left saying, "This looks really good. I love to read, but I can't afford it right now"… and then she walked away. About five minutes after she left, the LORD gently convicted me. I should have given her a book. I continued to look for her the rest of the day, but she never came by again. Talk about a big bummer. I began to ask God about why I missed this opportunity. In His still small voice He said, *"Natalie, you can't be prepared to handle things outwardly if you are not first prepared inwardly."*

In Proverbs 4:23 it reads, "Above all else guard your heart, for it is the wellspring of life." If we don't take care of our hearts we won't be able to be wise, full of grace, seasoned with salt or able to make the most of every opportunity that comes our way. So how can we take care of our hearts? I think of a gardener and how she tends to her garden (and if you saw my garden you'd know I'm not using mine as an example!) She plants her seeds—we need to plant God's word in our heart. Not only do we need to just read it, but study it. Understand it as we apply it to our lives. She cultivates the dirt to remove the weeds that will hurt her yield—we need to remove the sin that so easily entangles us and puts a barrier around our hearts. We need to remove the sinful things that can damage our spiritual walk and our ability to hear the LORD. She waters so that her yield will grow and thrive—we need prayer to help us grow and thrive in our relationship with the LORD. Take time today to prepare inwardly so that you are better prepared outwardly!

Heavenly Father, help me to walk each day through Your eyes and ears. Guide me to the moments, conversations, and opportunities that will lift up Your Holy Name by my words, actions, and love. In Jesus name, Amen.

—Natalie

Today God is stirring my heart by...

PRAY INSTEAD

"For in the same way you judge others, you will be judged, and with the measure you use, it will be measured to you."

Matthew 7:2

My husband and I were out for dinner the other night. We were kid free and so thankful for the quiet. No one was hanging on us, we didn't have to cut anyone's food, and we could eat without interruption. It was glorious!

After we settled into our meal, I heard some whining from a kid nearby. When it's not your own kid it is easier to block out. But the kid was especially loud and a bit obnoxious. I thought to myself "What is that kid's problem? Why aren't those parents doing something? Can't they control their kid?" I could feel my irritation rising as I sat there.

It was in that moment that the Holy Spirit whispered to my heart. He asked me to pray for the parents. He reminded me of the many, many times our kids whined when we were out at a restaurant or grocery store. The Holy Spirit also reminded me of the stress I have felt when other people hear our kids complain. I felt many emotions in that moment as I remembered. Those are the moments you do everything you can to get your kids to be quiet so they don't bother others and so you can have a peaceful meal.

The irritation within lessened and I found myself interceding for these parents. I had no idea what their day had been like. They may have not got much sleep the night before. They made have had a hard day at work with another co-worker. Their marriage could have been struggling. Maybe they just lost a friend or family member to cancer. This dinner out could have been the highlight of their day.

I had no right to be sitting there judging these parents. They were doing the best that they could do. The Holy Spirit convicted and challenged me at the restaurant that night. I am not a perfect mom and I never will be. I don't have the perfect kids and I never will. Instead of comparing myself to others so I could make myself look good, I need to get down on my knees and recognize that I need Jesus just as much. I confessed my sin of judgement that night. I committed to building other parents up in my thoughts and words. I also asked the Holy Spirit to help me remember to love instead of judge. And to encourage instead of compare.

Which parent have you been judging? Is it the stranger at the restaurant? Or is it a friend or family member? Take a hard look at your life and ask the Holy Spirit to reveal to you who you are judging. I encourage you to let God be the judge. He is the only one those parents have to answer to. Please encourage and pray for other parents instead of judging them. You will feel a lot lighter. I promise.

Heavenly Father, it is so easy to judge others when they aren't doing something I think they should. Please help me to love instead. Help me to look for ways to encourage other parents instead of pointing a finger. Parenting is hard. I want to cheer others on in my words and actions in this parenting journey instead of tear them down. Holy Spirit, I need Your help and guidance to do this. Thank You. In Jesus name, Amen.

—Anastasia

Today God is stirring my heart by...

CLEAR VIEW

"It is not good to have zeal without knowledge, nor to be hasty and miss the way."

Proverbs 19:2

When my oldest son was born, he took his sweet ole time coming out into the world—three very long and painful hours of pushing to be exact. I'm pretty sure I deserve an award. In the moment, my husband and I were smitten and quite certain he was the most beautiful baby ever made. Now when we look back, not immersed in the moment, we can't help but laugh because his first few hours of life he had a cone head and could have possibly passed for an alien.

Sometimes when we are in the midst of a situation, we can't see clearly. Our view might be foggy. Often times we believe what we want to believe and we justify our actions, words, and thoughts, only to realize later that we reacted from emotions instead of responding with righteousness.

Have you ever jumped into a situation, guns blazing, without seeking the truth first? Have you reacted without first discerning the truth? I have. We can find this wisdom in Proverbs 18:15, "The heart of the discerning acquires knowledge; the ears of the wise seek it out."

Have you ever lost your temper and justified your words in the moment, only later to feel convicted? I have. God tells us in Proverbs 17:27, "A man of knowledge uses words with restraint, and a man of understanding is even-tempered."

Have you ever pursued something, only to realize later that you didn't seek God's desire and direction first? I have. God reminds us in Proverbs 15:22, "Plans fail for lack of counsel, but with many advisers they succeed."

Have you ever walked down a slippery path that seemed okay at the time, only to realize it took you far away from God? God knew we would, so he told us in Proverbs 14:12, "There is a way that seems right to a man, but in the end it leads to death."

I think we can all agree, we've all been there, done that. That is why God urges us each day to seek Him and keep our eyes focused on Him. He knows that we will find ourselves caught in chaos, in a moment where we will live through our flesh. Are you in a situation right now that God is asking you to step back and look at it through His perspective? To gain His understanding and knowledge so that instead of responding through your flesh, you can respond through the Holy Spirit?

Heavenly Father, I ask that You would show me an area in my life where I am caught up in living through the flesh and not through Your Spirit. Help me to step back, soak in Your Word and Your Truth, so I am better able to handle the situation before me. In Jesus name, Amen.

—Natalie

Today God is stirring my heart by…

DELIGHT

*"For the Lord your God is living among you. He is a
mighty savior. He will take delight in you with gladness.
With his love, he will calm all your fears. He will rejoice
over you with joyful songs."*

Zephaniah 3:17

Who do you delight in? Who is the person you absolutely love
to spend time with? When they call you, you immediately clear your
schedule so that you can spend time with them. Maybe there are
several people in your life like this. What continually amazes me is
that God delights in His children. God delights in you, dear one.
Our key verse today is one of my favorite verses of all time. There
is so much packed in here. Will you join me on this treasure hunt?

First, God is living among us. What a promise! Jesus came to this
world so that we could have eternal life with God. He made a way
for us to approach God at any time. In Hebrews 4:16, we read "Let
us then approach God's throne of grace with confidence, so that we
may receive mercy and find grace to help us in our time of need."
When Jesus left earth, He promised that the Holy Spirit would be
our counselor. In John 14:26, we read "But the Advocate, the Holy
Spirit, whom the Father will send in my name, will teach you all
things and will remind you of everything I have said to you." We
have the advantage when the Holy Spirit is living in us.

The second treasure we find in this verse is that God is a mighty
savior. Oh yes, He is! Jesus conquered death when He died and rose
again. In Exodus 15:3, we read, "The Lord is a warrior; the Lord
is his name." God is a warrior and He is always on our side. No
matter what we face in life we can be confident that we are victorious

because of the work of Jesus.

The next three treasures we find in this verse are all "He will" statements. I love that we can rest in God's promises. He is involved God. The first "He will" statement is "*He will take delight in you with gladness.*" Dear one, do you realize that God delights in you? He loves you deeply. God longs to spend time with you. He thinks that you are very special. Delight means to be pleased with and enjoy. God is pleased with you and He enjoys you. You are very special to Him!

The second "He will" statement is "*With his love, he will calm all your fears.*" God's love is steadfast. With that love, He will calm all your fears. Any time that you are facing a fear in life, bring it to God. Rest in His embrace and let God take away your fear. You will feel more peaceful. And you can completely trust God to take care of anything. He has a great track record.

And finally, "*He will rejoice over you with joyful songs.*" God sings over you. He SINGS over you. Isn't that just so amazing and powerful? God loves to sing over you. And not just any song, but a joyful song. God sings truth over your life and sow seeds into your heart of how much you are loved. Do you listen for His song over you? I bet it is absolutely beautiful, just like you, dear one.

Thanks for going on this journey with me through one of my favorite verses of all time. Isn't this verse so amazing? It's packed with so much truth and treasures. The next time you are struggling with something, remember that God is with you. Lean into the Holy Spirit and ask for His guidance. Remember that God is your mighty savior. He is a Strong Warrior and can handle anything that comes your way. God delights in you and He will calm all your fears. God rejoices over you with singing!

Heavenly Father, thank You for saving me. Thank You for being my Strong Warrior. I love that You delight in me. Thank You for singing Your truth over my life. I long to believe it more and more. Please help me to take You at Your word. Thank You for Your amazing love that calms all my fears. Help me to rest in Your love more and more. I love You, LORD. In Jesus name, Amen.

—Anastasia

Today God is stirring my heart by...

WHERE DO YOU FIND YOUR REST?

"Come to me, all you who are weary and burdened, and I will give you rest. Take my yoke upon you and learn from me, for I am gentle and humble in heart, and you will find rest for your souls. For my yoke is easy and my burden is light."

Matthew 11:28–30

So many times I find myself at my wits end, proclaiming that "I need a break!" Does that sound like an echo from your mouth? We are overcommitted, only have two hands when we could really use six, exhausted with no rest in sight, overwhelmed with life and the needs that continually surround us, and the fact that we hear "mom" about 153,279 times a day (how can such a beautiful name sound so annoying by the end of the day some days?)

Often times I find myself immediately going to my worldly things to find my rest… zone out in front of the TV, girls night out (did I just hear an amen?), read a book, shopping, games, leave the house (it doesn't matter where, just as long as I am away), or a sweet-glorious-doesn't-happen-enough nap. Now, there is nothing wrong or bad with these things, but sometimes we can put too much emphasis on these things or put them first before we allow ourselves to settle our hearts and find our true rest in the LORD.

God tells us in Psalm 62:5 "Find rest, O my soul, in God alone; my hope comes from him." He is encouraging us to go to Him first and through Him we will find rest. A rest that calms our soul, revives our hearts, and empowers us to handle what comes our way. It's not that resting in the LORD reduces my "to do" list or depletes the amount of times my name is said—but I walk away refreshed and strengthened from my soul outward because it changes my human view to a more heavenly and purposeful approach to the things I need a break from.

God's peace doesn't give us the end of our labor, but gives us a purpose for our hard work. This aspect is that we will receive rest in our eternal home. It says in Revelation 14:13, "Then I heard a voice from heaven say, 'Write: Blessed are the dead who die in the LORD from now on.' 'Yes,' says the Spirit, 'they will rest from their labor, for their deeds will follow them.'" When we meet our Creator face to face, we will truly find our rest.

Heavenly Father, You have simply said to just come to You and You will give me rest. Thank You for Your promises and desire to lighten my burdens by taking them from me, because You are gentle and humble in heart. In Jesus name, Amen.

—Natalie

Today God is stirring my heart by…

A PUZZLE PIECE

*"Ah, Sovereign L*ORD*, you have made the heavens and the earth by your great power and outstretched arm. Nothing is too hard for you."*

Jeremiah 32:17

Have you ever lost something and looked everywhere to find it? And gave up hope because it was nowhere in sight? Me too. The last time this happened God used my 3-year-old daughter Analiah to speak into my heart.

One of Analiah's friends accidently took home one of her puzzle pieces. A few days later she went over to this friend's house to play and the puzzle piece was returned. I slipped it into my coat pocket to take home.

After that, I headed out and ran about five or six errands. I pulled things in and out of my coat pocket completely forgetting I had a puzzle piece in there. A few hours later I picked Analiah up from her friend's house and headed home. She asked me where the puzzle piece was. I reached into my coat pocket and realized it was gone. Analiah had gone a few days without a piece to her new puzzle. She finally got it back and then I lost it. I felt terrible.

So, I asked Analiah to pray with me about the missing piece. I prayed "God, you care about the little things. You know exactly where this puzzle piece is. Would you please show us?" Analiah also prayed. We looked all around the van, in all my bags, etc., but did not find it. I assured Analiah it would turn up because I knew God would show us where it was.

A week later, I was pulling things out of the van and I found the puzzle piece. I was so excited! It was tucked under the driver's seat and honestly I don't know how I missed it. God is so cool! I couldn't wait to tell Analiah. As soon as I could, I showed Analiah the puzzle piece. Her response was "Jesus will never let me down." What? Did my 3-year-old just say that? I asked Analiah to repeat herself just to be sure and she said the same thing. I love how she was totally confident that Jesus would never let her down.

What an example Analiah was for me that day. Do I honestly trust that God cares about the little things? Do I believe that nothing is too hard for God? Oh, that I would have the faith of a little child.

How about you? Do you trust that Jesus will never let you down? Do you bring to God even the little things in life like a lost puzzle piece? I can guarantee that Jesus cares about all that is on your heart. He cares about every detail and longs to take care of you. Will you let God take care of you?

Heavenly Father, thank You for caring about all the details of my life. Every. Single. One. Thank You that You are there at any time to talk to even about a lost puzzle piece. Thank You for how You use our children to teach us more about You. God, I want to have a childlike faith. Please teach me how. I love You, LORD. In Jesus name, Amen.

—Anastasia

Today God is stirring my heart by...

THE LOVE OF
YOUR FATHER

*"I pray that out of his glorious riches he may strengthen
you with power through his Spirit in your inner being,
so that Christ may dwell in your hearts through faith.
And I pray that you, being rooted and established in love,
may have power, together with all the saints to grasp how
wide and long and high and deep is the love of Christ, and
to know this love that surpasses knowledge—that you
may be filled to the measure of all the fullness of God."*

Ephesians 3:16–19

My father passed away when I was eleven, and when I entered
my teens my mom met and married my stepdad. My stepdad is a
wonderful man and we get along well, but we did have some awkward
and frustrating moments those first few years. He had already raised
three grown boys and then a feisty and self-centered teenage-middle
school GIRL was dropped into his lap. I can only imagine the many
conversations my stepdad and God had about what he was supposed
to do with a daughter.

One day we were together for a hayride, he came up to me
afterwards, gave me a big hug and told me that I looked pretty
(mind you I was in an oversized sweatshirt, jeans, and hair pulled
back in a ponytail with countless pieces of straw sticking out of it)
and that he loved me. For a man of few words, that meant the world
to me… and it made my entire day.

God woke me up early the next morning, bringing this

conversation to my mind as an example of how we can sometimes relate our relationship with God, to how we view our relationship with our earthly father. Maybe your father is absent and that is how God feels to you sometimes? I can tell you that God is always with you. Maybe you are constantly working at getting your father to love you, so you feel the need to "do things" so God will notice you or love you more? Let me encourage you that there is nothing you can or cannot do to make God love you any more or any less than He does right now. Maybe you are afraid to mess up or disappoint Him? Maybe you keep God at arm's length to protect yourself from being hurt? Hear this truth, God is always working for your good, He will never hurt you. Maybe it's hard to have a close and personal relationship with God, because you don't know what that looks like? God desires to show you what that relationship looks like.

I don't know where you are in your walk with Christ, but I do know that God wants a true and honest relationship with you. He can handle your fears, your dreams, your hopes, your frustrations, your past hurts. God loves you, cares deeply, and wants to be your Father! He wants to break any barriers you have put up, wrap you in His arms and pour His unconditional love on you!

Heavenly Father, draw me near to you. Remove all hesitation, replace my fears with trust and give me a true glimpse of your love for me. Give me the desire to seek You for who you are—and want to be for me. In Jesus name, Amen.

—Natalie

Today God is stirring my heart by...

A 400,000 POUND ANGEL

"The LORD is good to those whose hope is in him, to the one who seeks him; it is good to wait quietly for the salvation of the LORD."

Lamentations 3:25-26

I love how God works. He cares about all our needs. Every. Single. One. No matter how small or how silly they need may seem, God cares. The other day God blew me away with how much He cares. Here's my story…

I headed out to meet a friend for an early morning walk. We were meeting at a school that had a path behind it. After arriving, I parked my van and waited for my friend to come. I had my pouch with phone and a headlight to wear around my waist since the path wasn't well lit. My friend arrived so I hopped out of my van and we started to walk.

There are usually three of us that meet on Friday mornings. Today, it were just the two of us, so I felt a little more alert. It seemed darker than normal too. So, I prayed and gave God my fears. I relaxed some and enjoyed the time catching up with my friend. We walked on and came to the college campus that the path ends at. We usually wind through the campus and turn back the way we came. When we approached the campus, a guy came out of his parked car and walked behind us. I was on high alert once again. It was well lit on campus, but I was still aware of what was going on. We kept walking and he headed into the recreation center on campus. I let out the breath I was holding and relaxed once again.

After we circled a part of the campus, we headed back on the path. As we approached one part of the path, I noticed once again how dark it was. The fear crept in. Instead of letting it overtake, I prayed. "God, the path is dark. I feel scared. Would you please send your angels of protection? Would you please surround us and keep us safe? Thank you LORD." I felt peace come over me once again. I knew God would watch over us.

As we got closer to that dark part of the path, all of the sudden, it was brightening up. I was amazed and also curious. I looked down at my headlamp around my waist wondering if God just really brightened that up. But, it was still a dull light. I looked over at my friend's light wondering the same thing. It wasn't any of our lights. Where was this light coming from? In that moment, I looked behind me to investigate more.

It was then that I saw my 400,000 pound Angel. God had sent a train at exactly time I needed it. The light on the front of the train was shining brightly and lighting the very dark path. God heard my prayer even before I uttered it. He had planned what time that train would leave. He had planned the speed of the train. He had planned exactly how and when the train's light would shine on our path. It was not a coincidence in any way. God cared very deeply about how I felt and chose to answer my prayer in a very powerful and tangible way. I felt so loved and cherished in that moment. He used a train to protect me and help me to feel safe walking down that path.

The rest of the walk I couldn't stop smiling about how God lit our path. I am still smiling about how God pulled through. God stops at nothing to show us how much He loves us. Do you see it? Do you see the ways God answers your prayers? The ways He perfectly times out things? Be on the lookout because He is at work in your life. God cares very deeply about what is on your heart. Will you depend on Him today? I promise that God will not disappoint.

Heavenly Father, please open my eyes to the many ways You are at work in my life. Thank You that You care so deeply about all that I am going through. Thank You for the many ways You care for me and answer the cries of my heart. Please help me be more aware of how You take care of me. Help me to see the ways You answer my prayers and stop at nothing to show me how much You love me. Thank You God. You are so good! In Jesus name, Amen.

—Anastasia

Today God is stirring my heart by...

A REFLECTING POOL

"A fool gives full vent to his anger, but a wise man keeps himself under control."

Proverbs 29:11

A huge struggle in my life is anger, especially toward my kids. I have this look I can give them that could melt steel. I consider it my super-hero power as a mom. However, sometimes that power is used not for good, but evil. My anger doesn't always stop at the glare, and that is where I get myself in trouble. When my blood is boiling, holding my tongue feels impossible. My voice rises. Sharp words are spoken. Frustration slithers out from my untamed tongue. My tone is disgruntled and my body language is tight and at times, cold. Let's just say it gets ugly really fast and I become the fool God is talking about in our verse.

My oldest son Jarrett put me in my place one day when I was upset at him about something. He had done something wrong and I confronted him about it. Everything I said was the truth and what he needed to hear. But when I was done, he all so sweetly looked up at me and said, "Mommy, I understand, but can you talk to me about it in your nice voice?" Ouch. Insert knife in chest and twist! God has been doing a lot of work on my anger over the last couple years and I have been so encouraged by the improvements I've been making. However, now that my kids are getting older, I'm noticing the struggles they also have with anger. It's like I'm watching the mini-version of me. And as I am correcting them, I'm scolding myself. I need to be that example for them, to show them how to handle a situation without allowing anger to turn into sin.

God gave us anger as an emotion, and that in itself is not bad, but what we do with that anger is the key. Jesus was angry many times in the Bible, but he was a great example of how to handle that anger and how to keep it from tearing others down. Are your kids a reflecting pool for you in a certain area of your life? Is there something in your life that you need to be a better example of? Talk to God about it today!

Heavenly Father, help me to be wise and under control when my emotions want to explode. Help me to walk in Your ways daily so that I can be a good example for my children. In Jesus name, Amen.

—Natalie

Today God is stirring my heart by…

THE
ULTIMATE GOAL

"I'm not saying that I have this all together, that I have it made. But I am well on my way, reaching out for Christ, who has so wondrously reached out for me. Friends, don't get me wrong: By no means do I count myself an expert in all of this, but I've got my eye on the goal, where God is beckoning us onward—to Jesus. I'm off and running, and I'm not turning back."

Philippians 3:12–14, MSG

What are your goals for today? How about this week or maybe even this year? There are so many things I want to accomplish in life. As I thought about my long list this morning, I had to check myself when I read this scripture. Too often I get so wrapped up in what I want to do that I forget the ultimate goal in life. I need to keep my eye on THE goal. I need to be positioned to reach out for Jesus every day, throughout the day. How do we do this? It's really all about our focus.

In my grade school years, I was involved in the Junior Olympics at a summer camp. I was part of the 4x400 relay team. Through this running experience, I learned how much I loved to run. And now as I look back on it, I can also learn some life lessons. In order to be focused, I need to reach out, take hold, and run.

What does it mean to reach out? In running the 4x400, I had to reach out to grab the baton. My teammate depended on me to reach out to continue the race. In life, I need to reach out to the only One who can always help me.

After I have reached out, I need to take hold of the baton so I could do my part in the race. If I want to succeed at anything in life, I have to take hold of Jesus. And keep that hold on Him as I run this race of life. Without Him, I will trip up and lose.

And finally, in order to be focused in life, we must run. In a 4x400 relay, each teammate must do their part. After they receive the baton, they must run. Standing there holding the baton is not an option. It is the same way in life. After we have reached out to Jesus, taken hold of the gift of eternal life, we must run. Run towards Jesus every day. Focus our eyes on the prize.

I'm off and running towards Jesus, how about you?

Heavenly Father, please help me to focus on the ultimate goal. Show me the ways I am letting life trip me up. Help me to reach out, take hold, and run towards You. In Jesus name, Amen.

—Anastasia

Today God is stirring my heart by…

A MINDSET LIKE CHRIST

"Do everything without complaining or arguing."

Philippians 2:14

This is the scripture I have on our command center, easily accessible to view! I had originally put it up for my children as a reminder when they start to complain about how I am "ruining their life" that God commands us to do everything without complaining or arguing. But funny thing, I began to notice that my words are not always as uplifting as they should be when my mundane chores begin to weigh me down. Laundry, unending dishes, bathrooms where little boys lose all capability to aim (seriously, how much bigger does the hole need to be!), more laundry, dusting, sweeping, meals... need I go on?

So why does God tell us not to complain or argue? It is explained to us in the rest of the scripture in Philippians 2:15, "So that you may become blameless and pure, children of God without fault in a crooked and depraved generation, in which you shine like stars in the universe." Along with that, God tells us in Philippians 2:5, "Your attitude should be the same as that of Christ Jesus." I don't know about you, but when I'm complaining, my attitude does not reflect Christ's.

So how can we adjust our thinking? Once again, Paul teaches us in Philippians 4:8–9, "Finally, brothers, whatever is true, whatever is noble, whatever is right, whatever is pure, whatever is lovely, whatever is admirable—if anything is excellent or praiseworthy—think about such things. Whatever you have learned or received or heard from me, or seen in me—put it into practice. And the God of peace will be with you." As I ponder on this verse I am reminded over and over again how blessed I am and how thankful I should be. It's all about changing my thoughts and mindset. Instead of complaining about my mundane chores, find the positive in them! I have a washer and dryer, children that need clean clothes, and have the ability to make them dirty, a dishwasher, these amazing little miracles called "Clorox Wipes," food to feed my family, furniture that needs cleaned, and a home and family that I am called to serve!

Heavenly Father, help me to walk in Your attitude daily. You have called me to be perfect, and a complaining spirit makes me fall short. Grant me the desire to seek You in ALL situations and keep my words, thoughts and emotions focused on You! In Jesus name, Amen.

—Natalie

Today God is stirring my heart by…

LOOK TO THE LORD

"Look to the Lord and his strength; seek his face always."

1 Chronicles 16:11

Nestled into a comfortable chair at the library, I was thoroughly enjoying the quiet. It was so nice to read without being interrupted. I was able to get through a whole page. This particular Saturday, I savored some personal time while our four kids were with my husband. As I paused in my reading, I gazed out the window and saw a dad park the car. And then he started to the process.

You probably are very familiar with this process. If not, I am sure you have seen it happen. The dad pulled out the stroller base. Next, he unloaded the bag of library books. And finally, he pulled the baby's car seat out. After settling the car seat into the stroller base, he walked into the library.

Watching this all unfold took me back to our early days. The days where my focus was completely on caring for my kids. As babies, they literally depended on us for everything. I remember feeling so exhausted much of the time. Most days I was just going through the motions and hoping to get hours of sleep that were clumped together instead of an hour here and there. Oh yes, I remember those days all too well.

Soon after the dad went through that whole process, he was back again. The dad proceeded to go in reverse order. Child in car. Empty library book bag in the car. Stroller base folded down and put in trunk. Phew! Depending on how much sleep this dad had the night before would determine how tired he was from doing all those motions again.

Oh yes, I remember those days all too well. Those were the days I had to depend on God's strength to get me through. Parenting is not for the faint of heart. It is exhausting. The days are long. And then you start all over again. The key I have learned over the years is not depending on my strength to get through the days. When I did that, I was always more exhausted from trying too hard and I tended to not be as kind or self-controlled as I could have been. Our key verse for today reminds us where we need to turn for strength. As we face each day no matter what stage of life we are at God's strength is available. We must get our strength from God alone. Our strength runs out and dries up. But, God's strength never does. Take hold of God's strength today!

Heavenly Father, thank You for the gift of parenting. Thank You for my children You have blessed me with. God, I cannot do this parenting journey alone. I am sorry for the times I have depended on my own strength. Please help me to look to You alone for strength to get through my days. Thank You that You are with me every step of the way. You are a good, good Father. I love You, LORD. In Jesus name, Amen.

—Anastasia

Today God is stirring my heart by…

GOD IS IN THE DETAILS

"Keep on loving each other as brothers. Do not forget to entertain strangers, for by so doing some people have entertained angels without knowing it."

Hebrews 13:1–2

This past fall I went to the city of Indianapolis and was standing outside waiting for the restaurant to open so I could eat lunch at 10:50 a.m. (because I guess city folk like to eat their lunch in the afternoon—sigh, mom problems.) Right in front of me, sitting on the ground was a homeless woman holding a sign that said she was homeless and hungry. At first I felt very awkward, mostly because when I would look at her she was staring back at me, down to my very soul. I kept hearing God whisper the verse above, challenging me to what I would do if that was Him sitting there and how I could make this a moment that could impact His Kingdom. Obeying, but not completely sure what was going to happen, I began my trek down the concrete stairs, as God told me what to say and do. I gave the woman money, introduced myself (and she did as well), we talked for a bit, and then I prayed over her, telling her how much God loved her and that He cared about each and every detail of her life.

And today, that's what I feel God wants me to tell you. God loves you so incredibly much and cares about each and every detail of your life. He is there in your finances, the unknown of your future, in your marriage that is crumbling down around you, the exhausting days, the hopeless nights, the lost items, the crushing news, the hurtful words, the what ifs, the answered and unanswered prayers, your hopes, your dreams, your desires and your circumstances. You are cherished, adored, and priceless to the King of Kings and LORD of LORDS. God not only cares about the details of your life, but He is IN the details.

In Matthew 10:29 Jesus says, "Are not two sparrows sold for a penny? Yet not one of them will fall to the ground apart from the will of your Father." God is aware of everything that happens, even sparrows, and you are far more valuable to Him than they are. God has shown His faithfulness throughout time. With Noah he gave exact measurements for the ark. With Joseph he gave him dreams that would one day lead him to great leadership. With Daniel he shut the mouths of the lions. With David he gave him five smooth stones when he only needed one. With Jonah he gave a fish to swallow him to keep him safe. None of these men led easy lives or skirted around hardships or failures, but God cared about each detail of their lives and was in the midst of those details.

The more intimate we become with God, the more details we will see affected by Him. Be encouraged today that you wanted, loved and God does have His eyes on you!!

Heavenly Father, in Your word You tell me that Your eyes are on those who fear You, on those whose hope is in Your unfailing love. Thank You for being in the midst of each detail of my life. You know my ins and my outs, my strengths and my weaknesses, my hurts and my joys. May Your truths and unfailing love wrap around me today as I fall into Your open arms. In Jesus name, Amen.

—Natalie

Today God is stirring my heart by…

KEEP TRYING

"Let perseverance finish its work so that you may be mature and complete, not lacking anything."

James 1:4

Strike. Nothing. Strike. Nothing. "Mooooom!! I can't do this!" whined my daughter Analiah in frustration. It was lunch time and Analiah really wanted to light the candle on our Advent log. She could not get the match to light. Analiah had one too many strikes and wanted to give up. Her shoulders slumped and tears threatened to fall.

It was in this moment that I stepped in. "You can do this, Analiah. You have done before. Try it again!" I encouraged. She looked at me a little doubtful but tried again. Strike. Nothing. Once again I cheered for her and then she asked me to help. I assisted her in lighting the candle but I didn't do it for her. Strike. "Mommy, I did it! I can light the candles now!!" cheered Analiah. The excitement was contagious! There were big smiles all around the kitchen table. I was so proud of Analiah for pushing through and told her so. Analiah squared her shoulders and puffed up at my words. The rest of our lunch continued as we watched the flames of the fire dance on top of the advent candles.

In that moment, I had a greater understanding of God's heart for me, His daughter. How many times over the course of my life have I tried something and failed? I've whined and complained at God "I can't do this! I don't want to do this!" Sometimes I wonder why I even try. But, God in His infinite wisdom and patience, lovingly encourages to keep trying. God knows I can do it and doesn't give up on me. When I cry out for Him to help me, God is always there to help me. And sometimes like I did with Analiah, God assists me only a little bit because He knows that I can do it on my own.

One recent example has been getting back into running. This

past year was a tough year of injuries for me. While training for a half marathon in June, I developed plantar fasciitis in my right foot. I was off for three weeks and then started up again. It was completely humbling since I had to take it slow. Then, I sustained a concussion at the end of June and was off running for nine weeks. When I was finally able to get back into running, I literally had to start back at square one. I did the Couch to 5K program again. It was hard. I cried. I whined. I was winded. I didn't want to do it. I didn't think I could keep going. But, God knew I could do it. He encouraged me. God helped me by pouring strength into me. He asked me to be obedient and run. I'm so glad I didn't give up!

How about you? Where do you need to keep trying? Ask God to help you!

Heavenly Father, thank You that You are always there when I need help. Thank You for cheering me on. Thank You for meeting me at my worst and believing in me. Please help me to turn to You and keep trying. In Jesus name, Amen.

—Anastasia

Today God is stirring my heart by…

WATER TO
THE SOUL

"Like cold water to a weary soul is good news from a distant land."

Proverbs 25:25

After college, I lived in Ecuador for six months doing missions work as an English teacher. Email had just come out a few years prior and wasn't very popular yet. Oh my word, have I just aged myself?!? I feel like an eighty year old man telling of the good old days. I digress. In the city where I lived, I would have to go to the internet café in the mall and wait around forever for a free computer in hopes that someone wrote me. I can't tell you the happiness that filled my heart when I recognized a name in my inbox. I would soak in their words, sometimes print them out so I could read them whenever I wanted, and then smile or cry (depending on the day I was having) the entire time as I wrote my response.

I don't know about you, but I often think of reaching out to family and friends that I don't keep in contact with as much anymore. Many times God gives me a little nudge to be more intentional about making contact and speaking love and truth into their lives. To just send them a text or call them with a word of encouragement, letting them know I'm thinking and praying for them.

The other night I sent out a text to my college roommates that I haven't talked to in a really long time and we ended up texting back and forth for hours reminiscing, sending each other old pictures (of very poor haircuts, I might add) and just reconnecting. It was water to my soul.

Our verse reminds me of Paul and his letters to the churches. I can only imagine the excitement they had when his letters arrived. Just think of the encouragement they brought with the truth he spoke, knowing he was praying for them, and how their lives changed because of them. I've been trying lately to be more diligent in my prayer life by asking God to bring someone to mind that I can reach out to—and then actually follow through. Why is that important? Because God says in Proverbs 25:11, "A word aptly spoken is like apples of gold in settlings of silver." I don't ever want to miss an opportunity to let God work through me. Is there someone you could reach out to today?

Heavenly Father, thank You for Your Word that fills my heart and is water to my soul on the days I feel dry. I ask that You would put on my mind someone that You want me to reach out to and speak the words of encouragement and love that they need to hear. In Jesus name, Amen.

—Natalie

Today God is stirring my heart by…

SCARS

"But I will restore you to health and heal your wounds,
*declares the L*ORD.*"*

Jeremiah 30:17a

Every scar tells a story. I am sure you can remember the story of how you received the scar. Many of you could even tell every detail of what happened that day. We all have physical scars that are visible from the outside. But, what about the scars that are on the inside? The ones that maybe only you know about and hurt more than the outside scars did.

The beautiful thing about the inside scars is that Jesus can bring healing to them. He wants to take away the pain from any experience that has scared you. Jesus wants to help us remove the bitterness, the unforgiveness, and the sadness we may still experience. Jesus is able. But, we need to let Him. Why is it that we don't let Jesus heal us?

My daughter helped me to see why the other day. I changed out the PJs for the kids to some warmer ones since it was winter time. That night, Micaela was very distraught about the pair she wore. She wanted the old pair back. I didn't quite understand why. Honestly, I was a little annoyed with her about it. Micaela finally explained that she liked her Hello Kitty PJ shirt because she could feel her scab.

That got me thinking. How often do we like to feel our scabs that often turn into scars? The scars then become such a part of us that it's hard to let go. We don't want to let go of our scars because they become our identity. We feel as though we have to hold on to them. We justify our actions or how we see ourselves because of our scars. We believe what others say about us because they wounded us, so then it must be true.

As a youth, I would have never said I was beautiful. In fact, I was told by a few people that I was not very pretty. So, that is what I choose to believe. This is heartbreaking because the truth is that I am beautiful because God created me. I am fearfully and wonderfully made. It took until I was a freshman in college to finally believe the truth that I am beautiful. I let what others say about me define me. My scars do not define me.

The truth is our identity is in Jesus alone, not in our scars. Let me say that again. Our identity is in Jesus alone. And He wants to heal every one of our scars. Jesus came so that we could have wholeness and eternal life. Will you release your scars to Jesus? Will you let Him alone be your identity? It takes time and it is scary to let go. But, Jesus is with you every step of the way.

Let the healing begin.

Heavenly Father, thank You that You are my identity. Please forgive me for the times I have put my identity in my scars. Jesus, I give You my scars and ask that You will heal them. Thank You for being with me each step towards healing. God, I want to be whole. Thank You for healing me. In Jesus name, Amen.

—Anastasia

Today God is stirring my heart by...

FORGIVE
AND FORGET

"He said to them, "When you pray, say: 'Father hallowed be your name, your kingdom come. Give us each day our daily bread. Forgive us our sins, for we also forgive everyone who sins against us. And lead us not into temptation.'"

Luke 11: 2–4

When God gives us the example of prayer, He reminds us to forgive others. It's right there in the bold red lettering. We can't deny it. God reminds us that we should forgive *everyone* who sins against us. Gulp. How often do we forgive the tiny issues but become stuck on the big issues, the ones that cut deep? How many times have we messed up and realized that we have to work on forgiving ourselves also?

Why is forgiveness so hard? Because it's not natural. We were born with a sinful nature and our flesh fights against it every single day. We are only able to truly forgive though Christ. God forgives us and makes our slate clean, so who are we to not forgive others? I get it, forgiveness isn't easy, and that's what makes it a gift. Maybe the person you need to forgive hasn't asked for it. Or maybe you feel the person you need to forgive doesn't deserve it… but then again, we don't really deserve it either. Here is the clincher, the big "Ah-ha moment" (at least for me)… If we can't forgive others, can we really understand how deeply we need the LORD's forgiveness?

Ask God to search your heart to identify if there is forgiveness you need to give. And as I sit here and pray over these words I'm writing, I have to think that maybe that person is you. Are you struggling to let go of your baggage, your failures, and your shortcomings? We are often the hardest on ourselves and our own worst critic. We can't get over what we have done and replay what we have done over and over again in our mind, mentally beating ourselves up for doing something wrong. Don't hold on to your guilt and shame. God wants to help you release the bondage! You don't have to carry it around any longer—give it to God!

Oh Heavenly Father, I am a sinner deeply in need of your forgiveness. Thank you for Your Grace full of redeeming love. Search my heart LORD; bring to my attention anyone that I have allowed to come between us because of my difficulty with forgiveness. Give me the courage and power to approach and change the circumstances I can and the peace and strength to lay it at Your feet when I cannot. In Jesus name, Amen.

—Natalie

Today God is stirring my heart by…

ALL MY MIGHT

"But you, God, shield me on all sides; You ground my feet, you lift my head high; With all my might I shout up to God, His answers thunder from the holy mountain."

Psalm 3:3–4

Betrayal. Do you feel that heaviness in your gut just by reading that word? A story is probably coming to mind of how you were betrayed and the emotions of that time are flooding in. Can you imagine being betrayed by your own child? In our key verses for today King David, the author of this psalm, was on the run from his own son, Absalom.

Absalom had formed a conspiracy against King David to take his crown and his life. King David understood what it meant to be betrayed. Yet even in the middle of this betrayal, David wrote this psalm. He chose to run to God instead of run away from Him. David chose to trust God even in his heartache. How can we do the same? We need to focus on the character and consistency of God instead of our circumstances.

David believed God was his shield. He trusted the promise in Genesis 15:1—After this, the word of the LORD came to Abram in a vision: "Do not be afraid, Abram. I am your shield, your very great reward." David recognized that God was not only a shield for him, but a shield around him. God covered David on all sides. The King of Kings is your shield. He also covers you on all sides.

God can ground our feet and He lift our heads in every circumstance. As David hid from his son Absalom and the men who wanted to kill him, he had a choice. David could be discouraged and focus on his troubles or he could rest in the promise that God would lift his head and bring joy. David chose to trust God. He had seen time and time again how God used tough situations for His glory. God had provided and protected David on many occasions. David knew he could trust God's character.

In Psalm 3:1–2, David looked all around and cried out "God! Look! Enemies past counting! Enemies sprouting like mushrooms, Mobs of them all around me, roaring their mockery: 'Hah! No help for *him* from God!'" David was overwhelmed! Can you sense the helplessness? But instead of camping there, he reminded himself of what God's character. I love how David responds to God's faithfulness. He shouted with ALL his might up to God. David depended heavily on God to get him out of this mess. As we read on, we see that God answered thunder from His holy mountain. Once again, God proves He is faithful. He cared about what David was going through.

God also cares about the battles you are facing in life right now. He is there to be your shield on all sides. God wants to help you stand on level ground and desires to lift your head high. With ALL your might shout up to God. Cry out to Him with all that is within you. Trust God's track record and rest in the promise that He will answer you.

Heavenly Father, thank You for Your faithfulness. Thank for not only being my shield but for shielding me on all sides. Help me to trust that You will use all things for my good. You will lift my head high. Thank You that I can trust You. I love You, LORD. In Jesus name, Amen.

—Anastasia

Today God is stirring my heart by…

FOOTHOLDS

"In your anger do not sin. Do not let the sun go down while you are still angry... and do not give the devil a foothold."

Ephesians 4:26–27

I'm not a mountain climber. I've never even done a rock wall before. I take that back, I've "climbed" the one on my daughter Kyla's kindergarten playground that is only about five feet off the ground, and I might add that I made it to the top in record time. So obviously I'm not a professional, but I know in order to climb and make progress, you need a good foothold.

I looked up what the definition of foothold meant, it said, "a secure position from which further progress may be made." Wow, those two words, further progress, didn't sit well with me. God tells us in the verse above that we are not to give the devil a foothold in our life. I don't know about you, but I don't want the devil securing anything over me. Oh, but how many times do we allow him to do it or even thread our fingers together to give him that extra leverage and support.

And isn't that just what Satan wants, an inch here, an inch there, in order to further his progress in destroying our lives and leading us away from God. Maybe it's just a bad word here, a "you'll never believe what I heard" comment there, a judgmental attitude here, thinking you'll only do something once, or a spark of anger that so easily turns into a flame that destroys everyone around us. How does Satan get that foothold? It starts by our mind and heart not being focused on the LORD and then can turn into thinking that "just this one time" won't mean anything.

When God is not in our forethoughts, it is so much easier to have our thoughts filled with worldly desires and selfishness. That is why God warns us about giving the devil a foothold, because the devil will never be satisfied. And once the enemy gains that foothold, it will be that much harder to gain it back!

The good news is that we serve a mighty God that can help us. We can go to Him and confess the footholds we have allowed the enemy to have, and take it back! We are fighting a war that God has already won.

Heavenly Father, please open my eyes to the areas in my life that I am allowing the devil to have a foothold in. Give me the discernment to identify my weaknesses, break down my pride so that I am better able to hear Your voice, and convict my soul when I am not walking in Your ways. In Jesus name, Amen.

—Natalie

Today God is stirring my heart by…

PAUSE

"When Jesus heard what had happened, he withdrew by boat privately to a solitary place. Hearing of this, the crowds followed him on foot from the towns. When Jesus landed and saw a large crowd, he had compassion on them and healed their sick."

Matthew 14:13–14

Are you ever in a hurry? Me too. Sometimes too much. I get so zoned in on what I want to do that I forget there are people all around me. This morning, I was coming out of the store on a mission to get home and write. For this devotional in fact. I zeroed in on my van and plowed forward. Out of the corner of my eye, I saw someone say Hi and I said Hi back. Yup, I'm friendly like that. But then I paused.

In that pause, my brain processed who it was and I turned around. It was an acquaintance from my old church. Many years ago, I was friends with her daughter. After leaving our old church, this friend and I didn't stay connected but were always friendly when we saw each other around town. I greeted this friend with a hug and we caught up a little bit.

It wasn't just any hug though. This was one of those hugs that communicates that you care very deeply about the person and the heartache they have experienced. This family had gone through an extremely hard time when her husband passed away. The pain and questions were deep and are probably still raw even though it happened several years ago. It's not something you ever fully get over. That was "I care, I am sorry, how are you really?" hug.

All because I paused.

I could have kept going. I had a good reason to. But I didn't. Why? Because I desire to be more like Jesus. I want to learn how to pause and think of others instead of being so focused on what I want to do.

Jesus was always on mission doing His father's work. There was always someone that needed Him. He paused many times when He was tired, hungry, and worn. Jesus cared more about the heart of people and a relationship with them. In fact in, Matthew 14:13–14, Jesus had just learned of His cousin—John the Baptist's death. He withdrew to a solitary place. Someone who was very close to Him had died and Jesus was grieving. The crowds heard about where Jesus went so they followed Him. After Jesus arrived to the place where they all were waiting, He had compassion on them and healed their sick. Even in the middle of Jesus' deep grief for His cousin, He paused because He cared for these people.

That challenges me. That inspires me. That convicts me.

As I walked away from that time with this friend, I was refreshed. My step was lighter. Why? Because I paused to care. I paused to think of someone other than myself. I paused to be like Jesus.

Heavenly Father, please help me to pause. Please help me to not be so caught up in my life and my problems that I forget to pause and care for others. There are so many hurting people in our world. Please show me the people You want me to minister to. Help me to love and care for them as You do. In Jesus name, Amen.

—Anastasia

Today God is stirring my heart by…

IT DOES MATTER

"The sting of death is sin, and the power of sin is the law. But thanks be to God! He gives us the victory through our LORD Jesus Christ. Therefore, my dear brothers, stand firm. Let nothing move you. Always give yourselves fully to the work of the LORD, because you know that your labor in the LORD is not in vain."

1 Corinthians 15:56–58

Can I just be honest with you for a moment? There are days I just want to throw in the towel. Life is overwhelming, I have more things on my "to do" list than I have hours to get them done, parenting is hard, marriage is taxing, my work around the house feels pointless once my children step foot in a room, my prayers for situations and people feel unheard, I deal with lack of freedom over struggles, etc. Some days I just want to throw my arms up in the air and cry, "What's the point, God?"

I've been a believer all my life, my head knows there IS a point, but some days it just takes God doing some extensive massaging on my heart to make my heart believe it as well. Have you ever grown weary of doing good? I have. It sounds horrible, but I'm just being honest. Sometimes it's discouraging to give everything and continue to do right and yet see nothing in return or persistent resistance. God knew in our humanness this would be a struggle, so he gave us encouragement in His word in Galatians 6:9, "Let us not become weary in doing good, for at the proper time we will reap a harvest if we do not give up."

He also gave us many examples in the Bible to remind us that our labor in the LORD is not in vain. To God, every moment is important and every single person is important. In Matthew 18:12–13 it says, "What do you think? If a man owns a hundred sheep, and one of them wanders away, will he not leave the ninety-nine on the hills and go to look for the one that wandered off? And if he finds it, I tell you the truth, he is happier about that one sheep than about the ninety-nine that did not wander off."

As I bared my heart to God today, I felt like He said that in all the good things I'm doing, if they only affect ONE person, if only ONE person is changed because of it, I've done well because that is exactly what He has called me to do. Because that ONE person is that important to Him to orchestrate everything that surrounds that moment when their life is changed and their eyes become unveiled. And that is how He feels about you. I felt like God wanted me to share with you today that you are important. You are cherished. What you are doing does matter—you may not see results on this side of Heaven—but it does matter!! God sees you, do not grow weary.

Heavenly Father, You tell me in Your word to never tire of doing what is right. Help me on the days my spirit feels downcast to gain confidence in Your promises. Keep my mind steadfast on Your purposes. In Jesus name, Amen.

—Natalie

Today God is stirring my heart by...

TELL HER

"Therefore encourage one another and build each other up, just as in fact you are doing."

1 Thessalonians 5:11

As women, we love to look good. We spend lots and lots of time picking out the perfect outfit, jewelry and shoes to match. We want to be noticed even if we don't admit it. Women have a longing deep inside to be beautiful and to be noticed.

Unfortunately more often than not, we find ourselves comparing to another woman. Sometimes it's our friends or even a family member. We think and sometimes say out loud "I wish I was as skinny as my sister" or "Oh, I love her outfit, I wish I could have clothes like that." or "I wish I had her body shape" or "I wish I could sing or dance like her" or "I wish I could run as fast as her" or "I wish I had a life like hers because then things would be all better."

And if we are totally honest as women, we sometimes don't even tell our friends, family or stranger how nice they look. Why? We are so focused on ourselves and on what we want. We don't really think about the person. Sound familiar? It does to me too. I have done this too often. It's in these moments that God whispers to my heart several things.

First, He asks me to "TELL HER." Tell her that her outfit looks awesome, tell her than she did an awesome job singing or tell her that she did an amazing job on that run after working so hard. Tell her great job on eating and exercising, your hard work has paid off, tell her she did a great job leading that meeting at work. Tell her she rocked it on organizing her house, tell her that the activity she did with her kids was so creative. JUST TELL HER!! God reminded me the importance of encouraging instead of comparing. I believe that we as women need to just focus on encouraging others instead of comparing ourselves to them.

The second thing God whispers to me is that I am fearfully and wonderfully made. Psalm 139:13–14 says "For you created my inmost being; you knit me together in my mother's womb. I praise you because I am fearfully and wonderfully made; your works are wonderful, I know that full well." God said it so that makes it truth. I need to continually walk in that truth.

God also reminds me that He went to the cross for me and would do it all again because He loves me that much! In Romans 5:8, God reminds me, "But God demonstrates his own love for us in this: While we were still sinners, Christ died for us." I am valuable enough to God to die for. You are too, dear one.

And lastly, God reminds me that He is enthralled with my beauty. Look at this verse from Psalm 45:11: "The King is enthralled by your beauty..." God thinks I am beautiful. When I rest in full assurance of this promise and believe it with all my heart, then I can then walk in this truth. I don't have to compare myself to others, I don't have to focus on what I think I need. I can instead focus on God's love for me. I can be so filled up with God's love that it will just ooze out on others. I can focus on how to encourage others. I can JUST TELL HER!

So, the next time you catch yourself comparing, remember that God loves you, is enthralled by YOUR beauty and desires for you to "TELL HER."

Heavenly Father, thank You for loving me. I stand in awe of all You do to show me how valuable I am to You. God, I long to walk in this truth. I long to be confident in who I am in You. God, I am sorry for the many times I have compared myself to others. Please help me to use my energy to build others up instead. Thank You LORD. In Jesus name, Amen.

—Anastasia

Today God is stirring my heart by…

FREEDOM
FROM FEAR

"Even though I walk through the valley of the shadow of death, I will fear no evil, for you are with me; your rod ad your staff, they comfort me."

Psalm 23:4

Fear is a huge battle I struggle with daily. It could rule my life very easily if I would let it… and once upon a time it did for many years. Fear of death is a battle I fought in my mind each day. I know I'm going to Heaven, but it's the unknown, the how and when, that scares me. It's the constant fear of losing my husband, my children or those close to me. It's the torment of if I die while my children are still young, the difficult life they will live after… a life I know all too well. I used to have severe panic attacks and hyperventilate so bad that my face would be swollen for hours afterwards. I was once a prisoner, but I claim victory now.

God is not a God of fear and His promise is to deliver us from those fears if we seek Him. Fear can captivate and cripple us. It can hinder our growth with God and consume our thoughts, those very thoughts that are meant to be focused on God. Maybe there are times in your life where you fear failure, change, the unknown, or a new direction for your life God is calling you to. Maybe you fear man and what others may think of you. Maybe, like me, you fear the "what if's" in life or every aspect that surrounds your children.

In John 10:10 is says "The thief comes only to steal and kill and destroy; I have come that they may have life, and have it to the full." Satan wants our fears to rob us of the joy of the LORD. When we allow fear to consume our lives, we easily come up short in the blessings God wants to give us. When we live with fear in our minds and thoughts, it replaces the freedom and peace God intended for us. God tells us in our verse to seek Him, to go to Him for help, and only through Him will we be delivered.

What fears are you struggling with that need to be brought before God? Is there a victory that you need to claim over your life today?

Heavenly Father, I stand firm on Your promise of deliverance. May I always have the desire to seek You so that I may live a life that is full of inner peace. In Jesus name, Amen.

—Natalie

Today God is stirring my heart by…

A CARDBOARD TUBE

"Blessed is the one who trusts in the Lord, who does not look to the proud, to those who turn aside to false gods."

Psalm 40:4

The other day, my husband received something in the mail inside a long cardboard tube. Analiah, our 5-year-old, immediately claimed the cardboard tube as her own. I could see the wheels turning. In Analiah's eyes, the possibilities were endless.

Over the next few days, the cardboard tube was used for a spying scope. There was so much to explore. It was also used as a ramp. Analiah placed it at the top of the stairs and cars were pushed through. The cardboard tube was also used to roll marbles from one side to another with shouts of glee included. Who would have known a cardboard tube could bring so much fun?

On one occasion, Analiah was using it as sword. The next sound I hear was whining. After she calmed down a bit, I held Analiah and shared in her sadness. "What am I going to do now Mommy? It's broken!" as tears rolled down her sad face. After she calmed down some, I asked "Who can fix this for you?" Instantly Analiah's demeanor changed and she beamed with joy as she yelled "DADDY can fix it!!" She knew without a doubt that her Daddy would fix it for her. As soon as Jonathan came home that night, Analiah asked him to fix her cardboard tube. Within a few minutes, the tube had duct tape on it and was ready to be used again.

I love how Analiah was so confident in her Daddy. Why did she know that her Daddy could fix it? Because she trusted him. Why did Analiah trust her Daddy? Her Daddy has been a constant in her life since day one. He has poured into Analiah, loved her at her best and her worst, and would do anything for her. Analiah had watched her Daddy fix things around the house time and time again. She was confident he could fix her broken cardboard tube.

In that moment, I was challenged and convicted. Do I trust my heavenly Daddy like this? Do I believe God can fix anything? Do I trust that He will work all things out for good? Do I take my brokenness to God and let Him heal me or do I try to work with it on my own? God has been there for me since day one. Even before I made Jesus my personal LORD and Savior, He was there for me. God's character is consistent. He will never leave me or forsake me. God can be trusted.

How about you? Do you trust your heavenly Daddy? Do you believe God can fix anything? Will you take Him your brokenness?

Heavenly Father, You are good. You are consistent. You created this universe, yet You also care so much about me and love me deeply. Thank You. LORD, I long to trust You more. I long to bring my brokenness to You so I can heal. Please help me to turn to You for help. Thank You for being consistent in my life. I love you LORD. In Jesus name, Amen.

—Anastasia

Today God is stirring my heart by…

GUARD YOUR INNER CIRCLE

"Do not love the world or anything in the world. If anyone loves the world, the love of the Father is not in him. For everything in the world—the cravings of sinful man, the lust of his eyes and the boasting of what he has and does—comes not from the Father but from the world. The world and its desires pass away, but the man who does the will of God lives forever."

1 John 2: 15–17

We are to be IN the world, not OF the world. If you're like me, you've heard this statement many times before, but what exactly does it mean for us believers? First of all, it's easier said than done, isn't it! When we believe in God, death has no power over us. When we follow Christ, it changes our hearts and we should become less interested in the things of this world and have more desire to be like Jesus.

Over the next couple days we are going to talk about how we can submerge ourselves into the world and yet hold our ground. Today, let's talk about the people that surround us. Why are we here on earth? We are here to serve God and lead others to Him. Paul's ministry tells us that we are to make ourselves a slave to everyone, to win as many unbelievers as possible. To find a common ground, to not have a self-righteous attitude, to make others feel accepted, be compassionate to their needs and problems, and to live a life that looks different than theirs.

The trap here for many believers is when we make these people our core people. Now, please understand me. I'm not saying we can't be friends with unbelievers. God encourages us to be! But the concern is inviting them into our inner circle. In 2 Corinthians 6: 14 it says, "Do not be yoked together with unbelievers. For what do righteousness and wickedness have in common? Or what fellowship can light have with darkness?" I think it even goes deeper than unbelievers. We need to remember that believing in God is way different than living a life that glorifies God and having a relationship with Him.

So let's take a look at the people in your life. Who are you when you are around your friends? Do you change who you are when hanging out with different groups of people? Do you change your morals, values, language, music, television show and movie tastes, etc.? God tells us in 1 Corinthians 15:33, "Do not be misled: 'Bad company corrupts good character.'" What do you do with the people closest to you in life? You share who you are and you seek advice and wisdom from them.

Here are three verses that God explains to us the damage this can cause. "A righteous man is cautious in friendship, but the way of the wicked leads them astray." Proverbs 12:26. "He who walks with the wise grows wise, but a companion of fools suffers harm." Proverbs 13:20. "Stay away from a foolish man, for you will not find knowledge on his lips." Proverbs 14:7.

In your walk with the LORD, how are you being IN the world, but not OF the world? Are there any changes that you need to make? Talk to God about that right now.

Heavenly Father, as I immerse myself into the world help me to keep a strong foundation. Give me the power to be a light to those around me, instead of letting my light dim around them. Guide me to find the close friends that will encourage me to be a better person and grow closer to You. In Jesus name, Amen.

—Natalie

Today God is stirring my heart by…

WHEN MYSELF GETS IN THE WAY

"Do not love the world or anything in the world. If anyone loves the world, the love of the Father is not in him. For everything in the world—the cravings of sinful man, the lust of his eyes and the boasting of what he has and does—comes not from the Father but from the world. The world and its desires pass away, but the man who does the will of God lives forever."

1 John 2: 15–17

We are to be IN the world, not OF the world. Yesterday, we discussed about the people that surround us, our friends. Today, let's talk about the one person that always seems to get in the way. Ourselves. We live in a very self-centered world. It's all about: What can I do to make ME happy, to make ME succeed? What's best for ME? What's easy for ME? How can I obtain more wealth, prestige and power for ME? Notice a pattern here? Me. Me. Me.

So if this is what the world tells us, what is God telling us? We can find it in Philippians 2:3–4, "Do nothing out of selfish ambition or vain conceit. Rather, in humility value others above yourselves, not looking to your own interests but each of you to the interests of others!" Not quite the same, is it? And not only do I have to work on this continually for myself, but I also have to press it upon my children in a way that shows them how much I love them while explaining that life is not always about them.

My son, Brayden, gave me a good example of this when he was in

Kindergarten. I went to the school to have lunch with him and stayed for recess afterwards. We had a great time playing and then the bell rang, announcing it was time for the kids to get in line to head back to class. Brayden jogged up to the line and right as he found his place in line, a kid ran up and pushed him out of line and said, "Haha, I beat you. I'm first." Ladies, it about got ugly on that brisk April day on the playground. Mama Bear stepped forward ready to let that kid know how I felt about the situation, but I stopped when Brayden just shrugged and said, "That's okay. God says that the first will be last and the last will be first!" Bible burn. Not going to lie, I loved it and my heart swelled with pride… and then I cringed over what my reaction was going to be.

What a great reminder as we submerge ourselves into the world to put others before ourselves. In your walk with the LORD, how are you being IN the world, but not OF the world? Are there any changes that you need to make? Talk to God about that right now.

Heavenly Father, as I immerse myself into the world, help me to keep my eyes on You, so they are not on me. Fill me with a love so deep and wide that it overflows onto those around me. Help me always put You first and then others. In Jesus name, Amen.

—Natalie

Today God is stirring my heart by…

LET YOUR HAND BE WITH ME

"Do not love the world or anything in the world. If anyone loves the world, the love of the Father is not in him. For everything in the world—the cravings of sinful man, the lust of his eyes and the boasting of what he has and does—comes not from the Father but from the world. The world and its desires pass away, but the man who does the will of God lives forever."

1 John 2: 15–17

We are to be IN the world, not OF the world. God has created us and placed inside of us hopes, dreams and goals. It's exciting to have a plan in front of us. The world tells us to move forward, do what's best for us and acquire our plans and goals for ourselves. All our goals and dreams should revolve around one thing: Jesus. Everything we do, achieve, desire, work for—should be for the greater good of God's Kingdom!

We can't hide our intentions from God—He knows our hearts. In Proverbs 16: 1–3 it reads, "To man belong the plans of the heart, but from the LORD comes the reply of the tongue. All a man's ways seem innocent to him, but motives are weighed by the LORD. Commit to the LORD whatever you do, and your plans will succeed."

Ask yourself three questions when it comes to your plans/goals/ dreams/desires: Is this plan consistent with God's Word? Will it work under real-life conditions? Is my attitude pleasing to God? These are all great things to keep in mind when pursuing the plans

God has for you.

I often find myself going back to the Jabez prayer when faced with a new goal or plan, desiring God's blessing when I'm walking out in faith and pursuing His will for my life. 1 Chronicles 4:10, "Jabez cried out to the God of Isreal, 'Oh that you would bless me and enlarge my territory! Let your hand be with me, and keep me from harm so that I will be free from pain.' And God granted his request."

Let's break this prayer down. *Oh that you would bless me*—I often ask for God to bless me so that I can bless Him! *And enlarge my territory*—When I ask God to enlarge my territory, I ask that He would expand the number of people that I can reach for Him. That He would open doors for me to do His work. *Let your hand be with me*—When I am doing God's work, if He is not walking alongside me, then I am doing it all in vain. So I ask Him to guide me and direct my footsteps so that I stay in His will. *And keep me from harm so that I will be free from pain.* It is so easy to fall into the trap of sin. Satan doesn't like it when we are working for God, so I always want to be on guard and ask that God would keep me safe from sinful attitudes, thoughts and actions.

In your walk with the LORD, how are you being IN the world, but not OF the world? Are there any changes that you need to make? Talk to God about that right now.

Heavenly Father, as I immerse myself into the world, guide me as I make plans and goals for my life. Help me to be on guard, to stand firm in faith, be a woman of courage, and to be strong, while I do everything in love. (1 Corinthians 16: 13–14) Through you, help me to be all those things as I work at keeping in step with Your will for my life. In Jesus name, Amen.

—Natalie

Today God is stirring my heart by...

ASK FOR HELP!

"But you, Lord, do not be far from me. You are my strength; come quickly to help me."

Psalm 22:19

Which one is having problems now? I looked up to see who was whining and found Caleb, our 3-year-old, stuck and frustrated. Instead of rushing to help him, I just waited. I waited to see what he would do and also whether he would ask for help.

Our family fun activity this particular evening was using the bumper buggie cars. Caleb was having a blast scooting around. His joy was contagious. So, when he got stuck it was like his world was crashing around him. Caleb was stuck in a doorway and couldn't maneuver his way out. Again, I waited to see if he would ask for help.

After several minutes passed, which felt like 10 minutes, Caleb finally got himself unstuck. He was so proud but also continued to whine a bit because it had slowed him down. It was at this moment that I went over.

"Caleb, what happened?"

I got stuck.

"Why didn't you ask for help?"

I don't know.

Next, I explained to Caleb that he can ask for my help at any time. I am always ready and willing to help him. I also talked about how I didn't like to see him stuck. And then Caleb was off to use the bumper buggie. After playing while, Caleb got stuck again. He tried to get himself out of it, but couldn't. Instead of whining, he asked me to help. I was so excited to help him.

In that moment, I had a greater understanding of what God

experiences. He watches us scooter around in our bumper buggies of life. How often do we get stuck? How often do we think we can get ourselves unstuck only to get more frustrated?

Why doesn't God just rush in and save us from the pain? Why does He hold back? I think it's the same reason I held back from helping Caleb. I wanted to see what Caleb would do. God wants us to grow into stronger people who are more like Jesus. The hard times are what makes us stronger. We learn how to problem solve and get unstuck.

There will be times where we can't get ourselves unstuck without asking for help. We have bumped into something that is out of our control or we need the Holy Spirit to fill us to deal with a situation in a godly way. God is always ready to help us. When we ask God for help, we are showing our desire to build a deeper relationship with Him. We are declaring that He is the only One who has all we need. God doesn't like to see us stuck. He longs to help us. Will you let God help you?

Heavenly Father, thank You for always watching over me and caring about everything I am going through. Thank You for being my helper at any time and holding back when I need to learn and grow. God, I desire to turn to You more for help. I am so thankful that I can turn to You at any time. You are the only One who has all that I need. Please help me to depend on You more. In Jesus name, Amen.

—Anastasia

Today God is stirring my heart by…

BELIEVE

"Blessed is she who has believed that the Lord would fulfill his promises to her!"

Luke 1:45

What do you believe in? Who do you believe in? When hard times come, where do you turn? In our key verse for today, we are told that we are blessed when we believe that the Lord will fulfill His promises. What does it mean to believe? How do we walk that out in the day to day?

The definition of believe is: "to have confidence or faith in the truth of; to have a conviction that (a person) is, has been, or will be engaged in a given action or involved in a given situation." The three phrases that really stand out to me from this definition were: is, has been, or will be. We can believe that God will fulfill His promises because God is, God has been, and God will be.

God is. In Exodus 3:14, we read "God said to Moses, "I am who I am. This is what you are to say to the Israelites: 'I am has sent me to you.'" God's name is "I AM." We can believe God because He is.

God has been. God has been around. There was never a moment God was not there. Even before the world was created God has been. In Genesis 1:1–2, we read "In the beginning God created the heavens and the earth. Now the earth was formless and empty, darkness was over the surface of the deep, and the Spirit of God was hovering over the waters." God has an incredible history. God is trustworthy because He has been.

God will be. There will never be a moment that God will not be in. What an amazing promise! No matter what we face, "Jesus Christ is the same yesterday, today and forever" (Hebrews 13:8). We can always rest assured because God has said, "Never will I leave you; never will I forsake you." –Hebrews 13:5. God will be.

God is. God has been. God will be. Because of this, we can believe. We can trust that God will fulfill His promises to us. We can say with boldness "Yes, LORD!" even when things don't make sense. We can trust that God will come through in His time. We can rest in the assurance that God knows what is best. What areas of life are you struggling to believe in God's promises? I want to encourage you to lean into God. Study His character. Look for ways in the Word that God is, God has been, and God will be.

Heavenly Father, thank You for being You. Thank You for being there even before I was created. God, I want to believe You will come through. Please show me areas in my life where I am not trusting in You. Help me to surrender those to You and build my trust in You alone. Thank You that You never fail. I love You, LORD. In Jesus name, Amen.

—Anastasia

Today God is stirring in my heart by…

A SIMPLE
THANK YOU

"Now, our God, we give you thanks, and praise your glorious name."

1 Chronicles 29:13

How do you respond when someone gives you a gift that was unexpected? Do you respond with a simple thank you? Or are you like me who responds with "Thank you, but you didn't have to." God is teaching me the importance of receiving. He has endless resources and longs to bless and encourage when we need it the most. I believe that sometimes we get too caught up in our busy lives that we miss how God is looking out for us. God showed up in a powerful way not too long ago. He just wanted to remind me that He loves me.

We were on our way back from visiting our dear friends in Ohio. It was a wonderful time but we were all exhausted from the travel. By the time we got to a stop for dinner, I was toast. I was ready to be home and not be sitting upright in a van. I stood in the line at Wendy's while my husband Jonathan took the boys to the bathroom. The girls were with me and full of energy. They were accidently bumping into people in front of us. I worked hard to corral them. The boys joined us in line while my husband went to the bathroom. The level of energy went up. They were just being kids. But, I was tired and just needed a break. I didn't want to bother the other people in line but of course the guy behind me was accidently knocked. He assured me it was no problem. Jonathan arrived and took the kids to a table to wait. Phew!

As I continued waiting in line, the man behind me started to talk with me about life and kids. It turns out that he has 5 kids of his own, ages 15 to 23. He reminisced about the days when his kids were young and how important routine was for them. He also talked about how much energy it took. But, then he commented that he wouldn't trade it for anything. God used this man in line behind me at Wendy's to remind me what a joy parenting can be. And also what a privilege it is to be a parent. I felt refreshed and encouraged from our conversation.

The time for me to order my food was next. After I rattled of my order for our family of six, the cashier had a strange look on her face. She looked confused and asked "What did you say?" The cashier wasn't talking to me but the man behind me. He said to her "Tell them it's free." Wait, what? I finally understood what this man was doing. He was telling the cashier that he would pay for our meal. I was floored. This man had just poured encouragement into me and now he was doing more than that. He was heaping another blessing upon that. I turned around and said "Thank you, but you didn't have to." He responded "Don't take away my blessing."

In that moment, I was challenged. How many times have I taken away someone else's blessing? How many times have I said "You don't have to do that?" I need to learn to the power of a simple "Thank you!" I need to receive the blessing and gift that this person (and ultimately God) has given me. I need to be humble and grateful. I know I have a lot to learn in this area. How about you? Will you commit with me to just say a simple Thank You? Will you accept the blessings God wants to give you?

Heavenly Father, thank You for loving me. Thank You for providing for me. Thank You for using others to pour encouragement into me. Help me to be aware of the ways You are caring for me. LORD, I don't want to take away other's blessings. Teach me how to say a simple "Thank you." In Jesus name, Amen.

—Anastasia

Today God is stirring my heart by…

THE OLD IS GONE, THE NEW HAS COME

"You were taught, with regard to your former way of life, to put off your old self, which is being corrupted by its deceitful desires; to be made new in the attitude of your minds; and to put on the new self, created to be like God in true righteousness and holiness."

Ephesians 4: 22–24

I don't know about you, but I always look forward to a new year in anticipation of what the LORD has in store for me and my family. I also love the New Year because it is an example that life keeps moving forward and a reminder that I can't go back. I can no longer live in 2015. I can't say it's 2015. I can't write that it's 2015. It's over. It's time to move on and look ahead.

I also think the New Year is a good parallel about our spiritual walk. Paul tells us to throw off everything that hinders us and run the race marked out for us in Hebrews 12:1–2. "Therefore, since we are surrounded by such a great cloud of witnesses, let us throw off everything that hinders and the sin that so easily entangles, and let us run with perseverance the race marked out for us. Let us fix our eyes on Jesus, the author and perfecter of our faith, who for the joy set before him endured the cross, scorning its shame, and sat down at the right hand of the throne of God."

It's kind of hard to run forward when we are always looking back.

When I am trying to improve on something in my life it is always harder to make progress when I'm constantly thinking of the past and my mistakes. It's hard to make progress when I'm looking at what I did, instead of what I can do. That's why Paul tells us to throw off the things that hinder us. Take some time to pray and ask God if you have anything in your life that is hindering you from moving forward.

Praise the LORD for 2 Corinthians 5:17, "Therefore, if anyone is in Christ, he is a new creation; the old has gone, the new has come!" The old has gone, the new has come. Say that to yourself a couple times and meditate on its truth. Leave your old self, your mistakes, your shortcomings, your sins where God tells you—in the past!

Heavenly Father, thank You for loving a sinner like me, saved by grace. Show me the areas that hinder me from moving forward and keep me looking backwards. Move throughout my life this year, show me Your ways, Your direction, Your desires. Create in me a clean heart that throws off the things that hinder me as I move forward. In Jesus name, Amen.

—Natalie

Today God is stirring my heart by…

A GLIMPSE

*"You were shown these things so that you might know
that the L*ORD *is God; besides him there is no other."*

Deuteronomy 4:35

Being a parent is hard. Really hard. It is not a job for the lighthearted. Each kid does not come with a manual though I wish they would. Even though being a parent is hard it has also been one of the most rewarding and growing experiences of my life. I have never relied on God's strength like I do day in and day out with our kids. I have never felt closer to God than I do know. I feel like I know God's heart in a whole different way since becoming a Mom.

One of the key ways I get to know God's heart more is when my kids are sick. The other day, my oldest daughter Micaela had a fever, a very high one in fact. It was on a Sunday afternoon and she was worn out. I felt so bad for her and wished I could have taken the sickness for her. I wanted to so badly to help her feel better. The best I could do was pray and serve her. But I so badly wanted to do more.

Isn't God exactly like that? Doesn't He see us in pain and long to take it away? God loves His kids so deeply that He would stop at nothing to show His love. In fact, God sent His only son as the ultimate sacrifice so we could have life. In John 3:16, we read "For God so loved the world that he gave his one and only Son, that whoever believes in him shall not perish but have eternal life." God wanted to have a relationship with us so badly that God did all He could to make a way for us to live with Him forever. In Isaiah 53:5, we read "But he was pierced for our transgressions, he was crushed for our iniquities; the punishment that brought us peace was on him, and by his wounds we are healed." Jesus went to the cross for all our pain. He desires to carry our suffering for us. I love that I can get to know God more as I continue this journey of being a Mom.

Another key way I get to know God's heart more is when I discipline my kids. Often my kids make bad choices that hurt themselves and others in the process. And consequences come as a result of this. The consequences aren't always easy to administer but I know it has to be done because it helps the kids to learn. It shows my kids I love them and am willing to invest in teaching them.

In Hebrews 12: 5–6, we read "And have you completely forgotten this word of encouragement that addresses you as a father addresses his son? It says, "My son, do not make light of the LORD's discipline, and do not lose heart when he rebukes you, because the LORD disciplines the one he loves, and he chastens everyone he accepts as his son." God disciplines us because He loves us. When we ask, God makes us aware of areas in our life that need to be refined so that we can become more like Jesus. God is invested in us as His kids. God will stop at nothing to show His love for us.

What ways have you been able to get to know God better since you became a Mom?

Heavenly Father, being a Mom is hard. Really hard. Thank you that I don't have to do it alone. Please help me to tap into Your wisdom more. Thank for You not giving up on me. Help me to continue to fight the good fight and love my kids as You love me. In Jesus name, Amen.

—Anastasia

Today God is stirring my heart by...

GOOD FATHER

"For the Lord *God is a sun and shield; the* Lord *bestows favor and honor; no good thing does he withhold from those whose walk is blameless."*

Psalm 84:11

My daughter Kyla has a sweet tooth. If I would let her, I'm pretty sure she would just eat sugar for every meal and snack. But seriously, can you blame her? I'd love to have a cookie three times a day, too. In turn, we have to monitor how much she has throughout the week, and have rules set up for how much she can have. One day she asked me if she could have a piece of candy. I told her I would think about it and let her know. In her five-year-old squeaky little voice she replied, "Okay, but when you're done thinking about it, can your answer be yes and not no?"

It's hard to explain to a small child that even though something is good, doesn't always mean that it is the best for you. Because I love my daughter, I know that letting her have what she wants all the time or twenty pieces of candy a day is not good for her. God knows that for us as well. It can be hard for us to understand at times this idea as well… our best and God's best might be different, but His is always better.

There are many different ways we can feel God is holding out on us. We live in a world that never has enough and always wants something bigger and better, which will always turn into discontentment. I think the foundation of discontentment is when we feel we deserve more than what we have or God is not meeting our needs. But that's just not true. I heard a quote once that has really stuck with me. *"If He doesn't meet it; you didn't need it!"* And how do we know that? Because God has told us, even more, He has promised that He bestows favor and honor and will not withhold any good thing from those whose walk is blameless.

During the Sermon on the Mount, Jesus tells us in Matthew 6:26, "Look at the birds of the air; they do not sow or reap or store away in barns, and yet your heavenly Father feeds them. Are you not much more valuable than they?" God loves you so incredibly much. He wants and desires the very best for you. Just like my daughter's mindset, we can catch ourselves thinking we know what's better for us than God does. Sometimes it is hard to grasp when we're walking through a struggle, or not reaching a goal or dream, or not having earthly securities that He is not withholding the good He has promised. However, God sees the bigger picture. And honestly, the bigger picture isn't even about us, it's about God's Kingdom. Be encouraged today that we serve a good Father that always gives us His very best!

Heavenly Father, You are so good and I thank You that You will never withhold any good from me. In fact, You even say that You will work all things out for the good of those that love You. Thank You for always wanting the very best for me. In Jesus name, Amen.

—Natalie

Today God is stirring my heart by...

SAME POWER

"I pray that the eyes of your heart may be enlightened in order that you may know… his incomparably great power for us who believe. That power is the same as the mighty strength he exerted when he raised Christ from the dead and seated him at his right hand in the heavenly realms."

Ephesians 1:18–20

Do you have a song that you listen to over and over? One of my current favorite songs has a line that goes something like this: The same power that rose Jesus from the grave lives in us.

Not beside us, not in front of us but INSIDE us. When I hear that, I get so pumped up. The same power lives in us!!

That same power was the strong east wind that pushed back the Red Sea so the Israelites could walk across on dry land. They were able to escape from the Egyptians.

And then, that same power in Joshua was what obliterated the walls of Jericho with the sound of a trumpet. Those walls were the city's glory. And in the name of the Lord, those walls came tumbling down.

The same power in 1 Samuel was how David could stand before the giant Goliath. He came with a sling shot and 5 smooth stones. It wasn't the stone that knocked the giant to the ground. Even David said, "I come before you in the name of the LORD almighty." It was that same power that conquered the giant Goliath.

And then, that same power in Esther was what moved the heart of King Xerxes. Esther went before the King without being invited.

The punishment for that was death. But, God moved in the heart of the King Xerxes and he received Esther. Because of that, the whole nation of Israel was saved. That same power!

Throughout the Psalms, that same power of God is displayed. In Psalm 29, we read about how awesome God is. The voice of the LORD is over the waters; the glory of God thunders. In verse 4–5, we read that the voice of the LORD is powerful, it is majestic. His voice breaks the cedars. In verse 7, we read "The voice of the LORD strikes like lightening and shakes the dessert." In verse 9, we read that God's voice twists the oak trees. Have you seen an oak lately? God can twist it. That's amazing!! In verse 9, we see another display of God's power. "The LORD sits enthroned over the flood. He is enthroned as King forever!!"

Psalm 143:5 states "Great is the LORD and most worthy of praise; his greatness no one can fathom." We serve a mighty and powerful God. The Bible is filled with many more stories of God's awesome power. But the greatest work of all is when God sent Jesus as a sacrifice for us. The Israelites went from Shore to Shore. With Jesus, we can go from death to LIFE! We are able to draw near to God. Thank you Jesus!

Do you believe that God can conquer the giants in your life? Do you believe that the walls in your life can be obliterated? Do you believe that you have the favor of God resting on you? It really is all about a choice. Choose to believe in that the same power that rose Jesus from the grave lives in YOU!! And because of that same power you can walk in victory every day.

Heavenly Father, thank You that because of You, I can walk in victory. Thank You that the same power that rose Jesus from the dead lives inside me. You are mighty and powerful LORD. Please increase my faith in Your power. In Jesus name, Amen.

—Anastasia

Today God is stirring my heart by…

HELPMATE

"Her husband is respected at the city gate, where he takes his seat among the elders of the land."

Proverbs 31:23

Over the last few months I've been reflecting and being intentional about ways to lift my husband up. God has been speaking to my heart that my husband can accomplish many things… Greg can be a hard worker, a leader, and great man with a strong character without me… but how much more he can accomplish, lead, and impact with me at his side cheering him on and lifting him up as his helpmate and biggest cheerleader. So here are a few things, we as wives, can help our husbands become the verse above.

1. Pray for him. For his heart, his dreams, his passions, wisdom, discernment, God's will for his life, etc. Ephesians 1:16–19 says, "I have not stopped giving thanks for you, remembering you in my prayers. I keep asking that the God of our LORD Jesus Christ, the glorious Father, may give you the Spirit of wisdom and revelation, so that you may know him better. I pray also that the eyes of your heart may be enlightened in order that you may know the hope to which he has called you, the riches of his glorious inheritance in the saints, and his incomparably great power for us who believe."

2. Lift him up with your words—by speaking them to him and to others. "The tongue has the power of life and death, and those who love it will eat its fruit." Proverbs 18:21. Bring LIFE to your husband. When you leave a conversation when talking with your husband or sharing with someone about him, have you brought life or death?

3. To be faithful and respectful to him. To be the woman he is honored to have at his side. "A wife of noble character who can find?

She is worth far more than rubies. Her husband has full confidence in her and lacks nothing of value. She brings him good, not harm, all the days of her life." Proverbs 31:10–12.

4. Be diligent and intentional with loving him. Look for ways to give of yourself selflessly in order to serve him. "Anyone, then, who knows the good he ought to do and doesn't do it, sins." James 4:17.

5. Instead of highlighting his weaknesses, come alongside him and use a strength of yours to compensate for it. Use the gifts that you have been given to help him become a better man. God tells us in Hebrews 13:21, "May the God of peace, equip you with everything good for doing his will, and may he work in us what is pleasing to him, through Jesus Christ, to whom be glory for ever and ever. Amen."

Maybe your marriage is struggling right now and doing any of these five things leave a bitter taste in your mouth. Then start with one, and ask God to give you the desire to do the others. You don't have the power to change your husband, but you can ask God, in His power, to change your heart.

If you are not married right now, I encourage you to not just read over this and think it doesn't apply to your life. At some point, you might become a wife for the first time, or again, and praying over these areas can help prepare you for marriage if that is God's will for your life.

Heavenly Father, thank You for my husband. Grant me the power in every area of my life to lift my husband up by words and actions. May I draw closer to You, so that I am so full it overflows into my marriage. Help me to see the ways that I can be a better helpmate to my husband and give me the initiative to make it happen. In Jesus name, Amen.

—Natalie

Today God is stirring my heart by…

THE LITTLE
THINGS

"Listen and hear my voice; pay attention and hear what I say."

Isaiah 28:23

Single Moms inspire me. They challenge me. In many ways, they are my hero. I honestly don't know how they do it. The other day, my husband and I were out to dinner. Before we prayed for our meal, we asked our waitress how we could pray for her. She asked us to pray for strength. Then, she shared her story with us.

It turned out she is a single Mom. She is working two jobs to make ends meet. This Mom rarely sees her older children. Her first job started at 4:30 a.m. After she was done there, she came to this restaurant and worked until 11:30 p.m. Can you even imagine? I was so exhausted for her as I listened. This waitress impressed me with how joyful she seemed to be. As we talked with her more, we realized the place she received her strength and joy from was Jesus. She knew him personally and leaned on Him heavily. What an inspiration!

As we continued our conversation, we told her about this devotional that Natalie and I were writing geared towards Moms. Her eyes light up. I asked her to share something that she would want Moms to know as they read this devotional. She said "Appreciate the little things." She went on to share what she meant. Earlier that week, she had arrived home after a long day of work. She was tired and ready to crash in bed. She found a note laying out on the kitchen table from her teenage son. He had written a list of things he had done for his Mom personally and the things he did around the house. This waitress had tears in her eyes. She commented "I could focus on the fact that I was tired or the fact that my son had taken all this time to not only do all this work but leave me a note." Appreciate the little things.

Another story she shared with us happened a few weeks ago. She was at work and it was drafty there because of cooler temperatures outside. When she was on a break, she texted her teenage daughter to share about her day and mentioned about being cold. Later that morning, her daughter arrived at her work with a cup of hot cocoa. Our waitress once again had tears in her eyes as she shared. Her daughter had taken time out of her busy day to come and bless her Mom. Her daughter cared about her Mom and what she was experiencing. Our waitress commented again "Appreciate the little things."

After this conversation, our waitress had to move on since she had other tables to care for. My husband and I both sat there challenged, encouraged and blessed. Here was this single Mom who worked literally all day and all night and she was pouring courage into us. Her life wasn't easy, she rarely saw her kids, but she was a beacon of light. She radiated joy and loved Jesus. The single Mom knew she couldn't do it without Jesus.

As we left the restaurant that day, we were challenged to appreciate the little things in life. We were challenged to pay attention and appreciate the small steps of progress our kids are making instead of focusing on how far they have to go. How about you? Are you appreciating the little things in life?

Heavenly Father, thank You for this waitress. Thank You for the way she was thankful for and focused on the little things. Thank You for the way you used her to speak into my life. God, I want to be on the lookout for the little things. Please help me to be more aware. I love You, LORD. In Jesus name, Amen.

—Anastasia

Today God is stirring my heart by...

GOD'S LOVE
IS UNFAILING

"But I trust in your unfailing love; my heart rejoices in your salvation. I will sing to the LORD, for he has been good to me."

Psalm 13:5–6

Failure at times can be my own worst enemy. It knows how to beat me up, drag me down and make me feel defeated. Many days I can allow myself to get so overwhelmed by all the things I need to get done, to be everything to everyone, and the unending chores. And because of those unrealistic expectations I put on myself, more times than not, I fall short. I think my husband hears from me about three times a week, "There are just not enough hours in the day!"

Do you find yourself at the end of the day frustrated over your lack of accomplishments or overwhelmed by the things that never got checked off your "to do" list? Do you mentally beat yourself up for not being organized enough, disciplined enough or frustrated from your lack of memory that depletes with each child? Because seriously, I truly think they suck our memory right out of us. While driving do you ever panic that you forgot someone and have to turn around and count your kids? No? Just me? Moving on then…

Some days I wonder what God thinks of my busy life and the things I consider a priority (I'm sure I break His heart when I am running around like a chicken with my head cut off all day trying to get everything done, and yet I have NO time to sit and be enthralled in His presence and His Word.) Or the fact that I am more upset over the fact that I didn't get the dishes clean, that load of laundry folded (that has been sitting in the dryer for two days) or the house picked up, than I am over the sins I committed throughout the day. Ouch.

This is why I love this verse above. That despite all my daily failures and shortcomings, God's love is unfailing! I'm not a perfect person, but I serve a perfect God that isn't done with me yet. I can rest in the fact that He loves me no matter what! God knows I'm going to mess up, that's why He sent Jesus. Thank goodness my salvation doesn't depend on my accomplishments or failures, but only because of the grace of His sacrifice.

Heavenly Father, I desire to make You my first priority. Help me to bring You into my day more and lay my schedule at Your feet. Remind me that these defeated feelings are not from You and that Your love for me is unfailing. In Jesus name, Amen.

—Natalie

Today God is stirring my heart by…

REFLECT

"But I trust in your unfailing love; my heart rejoices in your salvation. I will sing the L<small>ORD</small>*'s praise, for he has been good to me."*

Psalm 13:5–6

Life is busy. Life is full. There is always something happening and on the schedule. But in the middle of the hustle of life, do you take time to reflect? As you read this, you may even be thinking to yourself "Does she know how busy I am? Does she even realize that I can barely get a few minutes to myself?" Yes, I do realize that. I understand because I have been there. In fact, I am still there. But, I have learned a few things along the way. Reflecting is helpful in life. It's so important to take time to reflect. Why? Reflecting helps you remember, rest, and rejoice.

Reflecting helps you to remember. One of my favorite ways to remember is to look through my journals. I see the many, many situations God has given me the strength to get through. I read about the times my heart was breaking in two and how God comforted me and used people to pick me back up again. I read about the joy of giving birth to our children or someone I love dearly come to know Jesus as their personal L<small>ORD</small> and Savior. As I remember, I can see God's fingerprints all over all my situations.

Reflecting also helps you to rest. After seeing all the ways God has worked on your behalf, you can rest in the truth that He will be there through anything else that comes your way. You can rest in God's unfailing love because that will never change. His love will always be there to catch you when you fall or lift you up even more when you are overflowing with joy.

Reflecting also helps you to rejoice even in the hard times. Why can you rejoice? Because you know that victory is coming. Time and time again God has promised victory. In Psalm 20:6, we read "Now this I know: The LORD gives victory to his anointed. He answers him from his heavenly sanctuary with the victorious power of his right hand." It may seem hopeless at times but God is in control and has the final say. Regardless of whether you see victory on this side of heaven, you can rest in the promise of heaven. A place where "He will wipe every tear from their eyes. There will be no more death' or mourning or crying or pain, for the old order of things has passed away." –Revelation 21:4

Reflecting is so important in life. It helps you remember, rest and rejoice. Will you take some time to reflect? Write down a couple things each day that you remember God has pulled you through. Rest in the truth that God will pull you through. Rejoice because when you have Jesus as your personal LORD and Savior you have an incredible home to look forward too.

Heavenly Father, thank You for the gift of reflecting. Please help me to take time to reflect. Even in the middle of the crazy schedule, help me take time to remember, rest and rejoice. You are so faithful God. Thank You for being my constant. In Jesus name, Amen.

—Anastasia

Today God is stirring my heart by…

FILLED WITH THE SPIRIT

"But the fruit of the Spirit is love, joy, peace, patience, kindness, goodness, faithfulness, gentleness and self-control..."

Galatians 5: 22–23

Take a moment to mentally walk through your week and how you handled the situations that came up by being a reflection of the fruits of the Spirit. The conversations with your husband, the words you spoke to those around you, the way you handled yourself with your children, your boss, your friends. If you are anything like me, you averaged about 5 out of 9 in most situations.

Some days I get so frustrated because I truly desire to be all those traits, but I continually fall short. It is a daily battle because we were born sinful and these fruits are of the Holy Spirit. These traits are the work of the Holy Spirit in us. Our humanness drives toward hatred, discord, jealousy, selfishness, anger, envy, greed and sadly the list goes on. If we allow these sins to take residence in our hearts and lives, we leave no room for God and His goodness. We can't obtain these God given fruits of the Spirit by trying to achieve them ourselves. Instead, if we want these fruits to grow in us, we must grow closer to God, join our lives with Him and ask Him for help!

When I think of fruit, I think of the tree that bears it. In order to have good fruit, you have to have a good tree. In order for us to bear good fruit, we must have a good foundation and a source of drawing in continued nourishment. God tells us in Jeremiah 17:7–8, "But blessed is the man who trusts in the LORD, whose confidence is in him. He will be like a tree planted by the water that sends out its roots by the stream. It does not fear when heat comes; its leaves are always green. It has no worries in a year of drought and never fails to bear fruit." I love the part that says the tree is planted by water and sends out its roots by the stream. That is what God is trying to press upon our hearts. When we are founded in His Word (roots in the stream), we can draw continued strength and wisdom on how to handle the situations that come our way and to bear good fruit.

Is there a fruit that you struggle with the most? Take some time to stop and talk to God about it, humbly coming before Him, asking Him to help you in this area.

Heavenly Father, my desire is to become more like You each day. I pray that Your Holy Spirit would fill me so deeply that there would be no room for anything that doesn't involve you. In Jesus name, Amen.

—Natalie

Today God is stirring my heart by...

THE BEST PART

"Again Jesus said, "Simon son of John, do you love me?"
He answered, "Yes, LORD, you know that I love you."
Jesus said, "Take care of my sheep."

John 21:16

What is the best part about your day do far? I asked the cashier at my grocery store this question the other day. She looked back at me in surprise. "Umm, I am not sure about that. Let me think." The cashier close by her was also surprised by the question and said "Do I have a best part yet?"

The cashier I originally asked admitted that I surprised her with my question. After thinking a bit, she was able to come up with an answer. She responded "I arrived at work on time. In fact, I clocked in a few minutes early." I responding in an affirming way to her about that accomplishment.

The lady in the line next to me turned to me in this exchange with the cashier and said "That's a really good question to ask." Her wheels started turning. I think I surprised all three ladies in that moment. To me it was a very simple question. Their surprise and pause when I asked the question "What is the best part about your day so far?" really got me thinking. When did I start asking this question? How often do I stop and ask this question? Why do I even bother to ask this question?

My husband Jonathan was actually the one who started asking this question while we were out shopping or on a date. I'll be totally honest, at first it bothered me. I would think to myself "These are complete strangers, why are you asking them a personal question?" I also wasn't sure how people would respond. I realized after God worked on my heart awhile that I was more concerned about how I looked or my husband looked than I was about the person. God changed my heart and I now know how much God cares about the answer to this question.

How often do I stop to ask this question? I would like to say that I ask this question all the time. But, I will be totally honest. I don't ask every time but I definitely try to. I want people to know that they are important and valuable. I want to be a bright spot in their day by showing them that I care.

Why do I even bother to ask this question? To show the love of Jesus. When I take the time to ask this question and then listen to the answer, I am sharing the love of Jesus. I am reflecting His character. Time and time again throughout the gospels, we see Jesus stop, ask a question and then listen. Jesus genuinely cared about people. I want to be like Him.

As I walked away from that conversation with the two cashiers and the lady in line, I was challenged. I want to be a person who pauses, asks a question and listens. I want to show people they are loved and valuable. I want to be a bright spot in their possibly really hard day.

Will you join me in this mission? The next time you are out at a store or stopping at a restaurant to get food, ask your server "What is the best part of your day so far?" Watch how they react, watch the way they think and then listen for their answer. People need a special touch of Jesus. Be that light in their day. Be Jesus.

Heavenly Father, too often I get caught up in my own world. I have so much going on and sometimes it takes all the energy within me to keep my kids from running away while I am out. Jesus, I want to be a light to others. Please help me to pause, care, and ask people about their day. Please help me to be You Jesus for it may be the only Jesus they get all day. Please open my eyes and help me to love. In Jesus name, Amen.

—Anastasia

Today God is stirring my heart by…

IN THE DESERT

"Jesus, full of the Holy Spirit, returned from the Jordan and was led by the Spirit in the desert, where for forty days he was tempted by the devil. He ate nothing during those days, and at the end of them he was hungry. The devil said to him, "If you are the Son of God, tell this stone to become bread." Jesus answered, "It is written; 'Man does not live on bread alone.'" The devil led him up to a high place and showed him in an instant all the kingdoms of the world. And he said to him, "I will give you all their authority and splendor, for it has been given to me, and I can give it to anyone I want to. So if you worship me, it will be yours. Jesus answered, "It is written: 'Worship the Lord your God and serve him only.'" The devil led him to Jerusalem and had him stand on the highest point of the temple. "If you are the Son of God," he said, "throw yourself down from here. For it is written: 'He will command his angels concerning you to guard you carefully; they will lift you up in their hands, so that you will not strike your foot against a stone." Jesus answered, "It says: 'Do not put the Lord your God to the test." When the devil had finished all this tempting, he left him until an opportune time."

Luke 4: 1–13

This is the scripture where we read that the Holy Spirit led Jesus to the desert and He was tempted by Satan. I don't know about you, but put a cookie in front of me and it's gone within five minutes. I can't imagine being tempted for forty days! Satan tried to trick the Son of God. It just goes to show that the enemy will go to any lengths to work at causing someone to sin. This moment in the desert is also meant to encourage us and show us that we serve the one true

God that truly understands. When Jesus came to earth, He had the same trials and temptations, but He gave the perfect example of how to respond and resist the enemy. As I was reading these verses about Jesus being tempted, a couple things were pointed out to me.

1. Jesus was tempted first with His strength. When I think of temptation I always think of weaknesses as being the easiest targets, but how many times do we allow our strengths to become Satan's gain? When we have a certain strength, I think it is easy to overlook areas that might turn that strength into a weakness. Many times we focus more on surrounding our weaknesses with protection so we are not tempted or attacked, but we have left our strength unprotected.

2. Turning the stone into bread wasn't wrong or a sin, the problem was the motive behind it. Satan works on us that way. Trying to persuade us to take action—even good action—and use it for the wrong reason. That is where we need to check our heart against the Holy Spirit to make sure we aren't fulfilling desires outside of God's will or doing things for personal gain. Are you serving at church to be recognized for your good deeds or solely out of love for Christ and furthering His Kingdom? Are you working toward a goal because that is what God wants you to do, or because that is what you want to do? Are your motives pure in the actions that you take? In Psalm 119:36 it says, "Turn my heart toward your statutes and not toward selfish gain." Is God leading you or is Satan trying to get you off track? Take some time today and reflect on your strengths and weaknesses…and who is controlling them.

Heavenly Father, thank You for coming to walk among us and being the greatest example we could ever have. I can trust you because Your Word is true and Your steps are pure. You have gifted me with strengths that should only be used for Your glory and toward Your kingdom. Convict me LORD if I am allowing these strengths to be used any other way. In Jesus name, Amen.

—Natalie

Today God is stirring my heart by…

I SEE YOU

*"She gave this name to the L*ORD *who spoke to her: "You are the God who sees me," for she said, "I have now seen the One who sees me."*

Genesis 16:13

Do you ever wonder if God sees you? Maybe you wonder if God is really listening. Does He hear you crying out day after day? I know without a shadow of a doubt that God sees you. No matter where you are, God sees you. God knows every need and hears every cry of your heart. Every. Single. One. I believe that sometimes we get too caught up in our circumstances that we miss the ways God is caring for us.

In our key verse for today, we are jumping in to a quite a story. Hagar, Sarai's slave, is found to be with child. Hagar then begins despising Sarai. In turn, Sarai turns to Abram to complain and cast blame on him. In verse 6, we see Abram's response "Your slave is in your hands," Abram said. "Do with her whatever you think best." Then Sarai mistreated Hagar; so she fled from her." And this where we will focus today.

This story teaches us three truths about God:

God calls us out.

God notices us.

God hears.

Hagar became tired from her travels to get away from Sarai. She was sitting by a spring because she was tired and thirsty. It was then that an Angel of the LORD appeared to her. The question He asked her in verse 8 intrigues me. "And he said, "Hagar, slave of Sarai, where have you come from, and where are you going?" God in His great mercy called Hagar out in her sin. Hagar answers very honestly and openly to the Angel's question. She was running away from her duty to Sarai. I am challenged when I read this. What am I running from? What sin is present in my life that needs to be confessed?

The next truth we learn from this story is that God notices us. After asking Hagar to go back and submit to Sarai, the Angel of the LORD, adds that her descendants will be too numerous to count. In verse 11, "The angel of the LORD also said to her: "You are now pregnant and you will give birth to a son. You shall name him Ishmael, for the LORD has heard of your misery." God cared about Hagar and knew she was carrying a child. God used the angel to assure her that He would take care of her.

And finally, God hears. In the second part of verse 11, the Angel of the LORD told Hagar what her son's name would be. What an incredible honor for God to name her child. And do you see the reason Hagar is to name her son Ishmael? For the LORD has heard. God wanted to remind Hagar that He hears her cries. God cares about every single one. Every time that Hagar looked at her son, she would be reminded that God listens.

I love Hagar's response, which is our key verse Genesis 16:13: "She gave this name to the LORD who spoke to her: "You are the God who sees me," for she said, "I have now seen the One who sees me." Hagar experienced God in a powerful way that day. God called her out. God noticed her and God heard Hagar. God does the same for you, dear one.

Heavenly Father, I want to recognize these truths about You more in my life. Thank You that You call me out in my sin. Help me to listen, respond and make a change. Thank for noticing me and hearing the cries of my heart. Help me to continue to cry out to You alone. In Jesus name, Amen.

—Anastasia

Today God is stirring my heart by…

_____

_____

_____

_____

FOCUS ON WHAT MATTERS

"This is the day the LORD has made; let us rejoice and be glad in it."

Psalm 118:24

There are some days I want to hit the reset button before I even get out of bed. A long night up with the kids (did you notice plural). An early riser tapping my shoulder before sunrise wanting breakfast. A "to-do" list running through my head, feeling already defeated. The circumstances I know will confront me as soon as my feet hit the ground (Let me tell you, fifth grade homework might just be the death of me.) The opposition I will fight against with each step I take.

God knew how easily we would become bombarded with life and how quickly we can lose our joy. It's easy to get off track and let the struggles of the day bring you down. In effort to help myself and my kids keep our focus on what matters, I came up with a little chant we sing before school or when the day is getting out of control, or when we all need a smile. We sing, "It's going be a great day, because the LORD made it!" That's it. Simple, but oh so true. I love it because it reminds me that the day isn't great because I'm happy, my family is healthy, my marriage is thriving, I enjoy my job, we are financially set, I have all my wants, my house is spotless, or my kids are perfect. Nope. It's a great day because the LORD made it! I am alive to live out this day and what a great reminder to live it out faithfully to the One who created it!

The book of Psalms is full of authors sharing their heart with

God and being honest with Him, and then ending with praise for their Creator. I've learned on the days when my mood is low or situations feel overwhelming, I find a great peace when I stop and find a reason to rejoice. Sometimes I put on some worship music, or read scriptures that talk about praising God, or find a quiet spot and just rest in the LORD. When we spend time with God, He will show us the reason to rejoice in Him.

Heavenly Father, may I find my joy today in You alone. Thank You for this day I have to live for You, help me not to take it for granted, but to bring honor to Your name and kingdom! In Jesus name, Amen.

—Natalie

Today God is stirring my heart by…

I DON'T WANT ORANGE!

"And we know that in all things God works for the good of those who love him, who have been called according to his purpose."

Romans 8:28

I don't want orange!" whined Caleb after drawing a card. We were in the middle of an intense game of Candyland. Caleb was ahead of me but also determined to win. So, when he drew the orange card, Caleb was mad. That orange card was not going to get him to the winning spot. Caleb wanted to skip ahead and win. He complained and tried to draw another card. I explained to him that you only get to draw one card and you need to do what it says even if you don't like it. After a little pouting, Caleb finally conceded and went to the orange spot.

We continued on with the game and God started speaking to my heart. He gently said "You're a lot like Caleb. You want to skip ahead sometimes and get past the hard times." In that moment, I was convicted. How often do I complain when a circumstance comes that I don't want? How often do I desire to draw another "card" so I can avoid the pain? Way too many times. I need to take my own advice that I gave to Caleb.

This past summer, I accidently pulled down the van hatch door on the bridge of my nose. At first, the doctor thought I broke my nose. Since it wasn't constricting my breathing, there was nothing they could do. My nose had to heal on its own. In this time of healing, I experienced headaches daily. It wasn't your typical headache. It was worse than a migraine in some ways. After a month, we talked with the doctor again and said something needs to be done. We tried several things and the pain didn't stop. The next step was a CT scan. The scan showed no signs of broken bones or fractured skull. So, why was I still experiencing headaches? My doctor finally determined I was dealing with post-concussion headaches. The process of trying to heal from this accident began. This was one of those times I wish I could skip ahead in the game of life. I didn't want the "Concussion headaches and nose pain" card. God taught me a lot through this journey.

Even if I don't like the circumstances in my life, I still need to embrace where God has me. He works through everything for His glory. Instead of fighting the hard time, I need to lean into God and ask what He wants me to learn from the circumstance. Instead of wanting to skip past the hard time, I need to look for ways I can be more like Jesus in that time.

How about you? Do you find yourself wanting to get another card so you can skip ahead? Do you find yourself fighting God over your current circumstances? I encourage you to lean into God and open your heart to what He wants to teach you.

Heavenly Father, I really don't like the hard circumstances I am facing right now. Please help me not to complain or fight You on them. Please open my heart and teach me. Help me to receive the good You have for me in these circumstances. In Jesus name, Amen.

—Anastasia

Today God is stirring my heart by…

UNDESERVED GRACE

"All this is for your benefit, so that the grace that is reaching more and more people may cause thanksgiving to overflow to the glory of God."

2 Corinthians 4:15

I am not a morning person. I can't just jump out of bed singing praises with the birds as I start my day. I need to wake up and then have a few minutes to prepare myself and get my attitude in check. Sadly, it is a known fact at my house that if you wake mommy up to ask for something with your dragon breath, step back, because you have just poked the bear.

Well, my oldest son gets it honestly. When he wakes up on his own, life is good and he is great and happy. But if I have to wake him up, that is not always the outcome. One day we had a rough morning, and then on top of his out-of-control bad mood, he asked if he could have a friend over after school. The audacity! As a mom, my job is to help and guide him to become the man God created him to be. To discipline him, to show him what is right and wrong, to take care of him and love him. And along with that, there is a time and place to show grace. What I really wanted to do was laugh and say, (in my low, how-dare-you voice) "You'll be lucky if you EVER have a friend over again." Instead, I had compassion for him that morning because I know what it feels like. I prayed about it and decided that this was a time to show grace and turned it into a teachable moment. Once he was ready to have a conversation, I asked, "Do you think you deserve a friend over?" He hung his head and said, "No." I responded by saying, "No, you don't deserve a friend over. Just like we don't deserve to go to Heaven, but God has saved us and shown us grace so that we can. So I'm going to let you have a friend over, not because you deserve it, but for you to understand what grace feels like."

Now, just so you don't think my mom talks go awesome all the time, I'll fill you in on how it went with my second son. He disobeyed a rule, but still wanted to have a privilege. After praying about it, I decided this would be a good time to share a lesson on grace. I said, "Brayden, what you did was wrong and I know you're sorry, so I'm going to show you a little grace. Do you know what grace means?" He said no, so I continued. "Grace is when Jesus was hung on a cross to die for our sins…" and that is as far as I got. He gave me a terrified look and started crying with huge tears, panicking. "What? You're going to hang me on a cross?" Face palm. So there's that. Mom fail.

I don't know about you, but I am overwhelmed some days at the gift of grace that God gives me. And how we should often in our relationship with others, bestow that grace also. Is there situation in your life right now that needs your grace? Is there a person that doesn't deserve it, but God is calling you to mend that relationship by showing a little grace? As a mom, look for an opportunity today or this week that you can grab hold of to teach your child a lesson to help them grasp the gift of grace? Also, ask God to show you where your grace is needed.

Heavenly Father, thank You for Your grace that takes a sinner like me, and gives me the freedom and the gift to be forgiven so that I can spend eternity with You. Give me the ability to see what areas or people in my life need grace today. In Jesus name, Amen.

—Natalie

Today God is stirring my heart by…

A COIN IN A FISH

"After Jesus and his disciples arrived in Capernaum, the collectors of the two-drachma temple tax came to Peter and asked, "Doesn't your teacher pay the temple tax?" "Yes, he does," he replied. When Peter came into the house, Jesus was the first to speak. "What do you think, Simon?" he asked. "From whom do the kings of the earth collect duty and taxes—from their own children or from others?" "From others," Peter answered. "Then the children are exempt," Jesus said to him. "But so that we may not cause offense, go to the lake and throw out your line. Take the first fish you catch; open its mouth and you will find a four-drachma coin. Take it and give it to them for my tax and yours."

Matthew 17:24–27

Do you ever read something and stop in your tracks? And then, you go back and reread it because surely you read that wrong. The other day I was reading in the gospel of Matthew and I did that very thing. Jesus asked Peter a question and then he asked him to go fishing. I learned a lot about Jesus from this story.

First, Jesus knows our needs before we even ask. The tax collectors questioned Peter about paying the temple tax. Afterwards, Peter headed back to the house where Jesus was. Before Peter could even share about this conversation, Jesus knew the need. He asked Peter a question to get him thinking for himself.

Second, Jesus uses what is familiar to us to answer our prayers.

Jesus didn't want to offend the tax collectors of the day, so He provided tax money for both Peter and himself. How did He provide it? By asking Peter to go fishing. I bet Peter probably wondered why fishing? I think Jesus wanted Peter to do something he was very familiar with so Peter wouldn't be distracted by the details. Jesus wanted Peter to look for the answer and focus on how He provided.

And finally, Jesus always provides. He always comes through. In this case, Jesus used a fish. And not just any fish, but the first fish Peter caught. That in itself is a miracle. You don't see a fish with a coin in its mouth very often, do you? I love how Jesus uses anything to show us how much he cares about us.

Jesus cares about you also. He knows your needs before you even ask. There have been many, many times that God has provided for our family over the years. I love when He shows off like that! One of my favorite stories to tell is from our early years of marriage. My husband and I needed some toiletries and groceries. But, we were out of money until our next paycheck a few days later. The next morning, we woke up to a note attached to our front door and garage. Someone had blessed us with some gift cards to Target and Walmart. God knew our need and used this friend to provide for our needs.

Jesus will answer your prayers in many different ways. Some prayers He may answer using something very familiar to you. And remember, God always provides. He will come through for you. And who knows, maybe Jesus will use a fish to teach you a lesson too.

Heavenly Father, I love that You know our needs before we even ask. Thank You for using what is familiar to me to answer my prayers. Thank You for also for always providing. Please help me to be more aware of the ways You are at work. You are a good, good Father. I love You, LORD. In Jesus name, Amen.

—Anastasia

Today God is stirring my heart by…

GOD WILL LEAD YOU

"I will lead the blind by ways they have not known, along unfamiliar paths I will guide them; I will turn the darkness into light before them and make the rough places smooth. These are the things I will do; I will not forsake them."

Isaiah 42:16

I love this verse, and pray it over my life, during the many times when I am not sure where to go or which way to turn. During those unknown places when I know my desires and wants, but I'm not sure what God wants for me and where God is calling me. I obviously want His will to be done, because without Him my desire would be pointless. I don't ever want to be in a place in my life that has not been ordained by God.

Have you ever been at a place like this in your life? When you are not sure where God is calling you. It can be a very frustrating time. I challenge you to pursue God and His desires for your life. Ask Him to be your eyes, your hands, and your feet as you tread through this unknown time. That He would reveal His plans for you. That He would turn the darkness into light before you as He reveals which direction you should go. That your desires would become in tune with His. How does this happen? By spending time with Him, digging into the Word, and taking the time to be still so that you can listen for His leading. Isaiah 30:21 says, "Whether you turn to the right or to the left, your ears will hear a voice behind you, saying,

"This is the way; walk in it."

God also encourages us to get godly advice and wisdom from others in Proverbs 15:22, "Plans fail for lack of counsel, but with many advisers they succeed." You need to weigh their suggestions carefully with what the Holy Spirit is telling you, but it is good to get different perspectives as you make decisions and plans for your life.

Most importantly you must have faith. If you go into this time not confident that He will lead you, the waters will be muddy and you will be easily distracted or unable to identify His direction. Stand firm on His promise that He will not forsake you and in His perfect timing reveal His good—and perfect will for your life.

Heavenly Father, with You is where I want to be. I desire Your Spirit, Your presence, and Your divine calling for my life. Help me to keep my mind and heart clean so that I am better able to hear Your voice. In Jesus name, Amen.

—Natalie

Today God is stirring my heart by…

REACH OUT

"Therefore encourage one another and build each other up, just as in fact you are doing."

1 Thessalonians 5:11

My friends and I met for an early morning breakfast the other day. We normally walk on Friday mornings but because of the colder temperatures, we haven't been walking. So, we decided to do another kind of get together. It was a fun treat in the middle of our busy week.

We enjoyed catching up and just being together. I loved that we could encourage one another in whatever we had going on that week. That is one of my favorite things about these dear friends.

Our breakfast came and the waitress asked if we needed anything else. We thanked her for our meal. And then my friend said "We are going to pray for our meal. Is there any way can we pray for you today?"

The look on waitress' face was relief. She immediately answered yes and launched into a story. Her daughter is in the Army and was going overseas soon. She wasn't able to be home for Christmas. Though her daughter was excited and loving being in the Army, her Mom was not. She feared for her daughter's safety but also knew that was where her daughter was supposed to be. After sharing her story, the waitress reached for our hands, and said "Let's pray." My friend led us in a beautiful prayer for the waitress and for her daughter. You could tell it meant a lot to our waitress. As she walked away, I was encouraged and challenged.

First, I absolutely loved that our waitress reached for our hands. She obviously knew the power of prayer and wanted to be a part of it. Our waitress knew that God could calm all her fears and keep her daughter safe. There is something about joining hands in prayer in agreement that puts a big smile on God's face.

I also was challenged from that time of prayer. How often do I get so caught up in my own life that I miss the chance to encourage someone else? There are so many hurting people in this world that need the hope of Jesus. There are many believers who need a boost of encouragement because they are struggling with something. I desire to be more alert to those around me. I long to look outside myself and reach out to others.

How about you? Who can you reach out to today? It could be the waitress at a restaurant or the cashier at the grocery store. Or it could be the receptionist at your doctor's office that has had a very long day. Will you join me in reaching out to others to share the hope and love of Jesus?

Heavenly Father, please help me to be more aware of those who need You. Help me to reach out by asking about their day and praying for them. Please show me ways I can encourage and build others up. In Jesus name, Amen.

—Anastasia

Today God is stirring my heart by…

A HEART
UNDIVIDED

"Teach me your way, Oh LORD, and I will walk in your truth; give me an undivided heart, that I may fear your name."

Psalm 86:11

I have three kids, and oh boy do I love them. They often ask me, "Do you love us all the same?" And I always answer with, "I love you all very, very much and mommy's heart is made to love you all the same." As a mom, we are made to open our hearts and love our children equally, but as a believer, that is not the case. In the verse above God tells us to have an undivided heart when it comes to Him, and those words really hit me hard. I don't know about you, but I know I allow my heart all too often to become divided. Here is a question that I have started to ask myself and I encourage you to do as well: How often do you allow your heart to become divided when you watch a TV show or movie, the words you speak, the music you listen to, your priorities (are you putting something above your relationship with Christ)?

When I think of having an undivided heart, I also think about the verse in 2 Peter 2:19, "They promise them freedom, while they themselves are salves of depravity—for a man is a slave to whatever has mastered him." When our heart is divided that usually means we have allowed something or someone to have control over us. I've realized over the last year how much I've allowed myself to be mastered by my flesh. I truly desire to have a selfless faith, but in order to accomplish that I need to die to my flesh each and every day.

Jesus tells us in Matthew 22:37 "Love the LORD your God with all your heart and with all your soul and with all your mind." Have you loved God like this lately? I encourage you to ask the LORD to convict you on an area in your life that you are allowing your heart to be divided. I'll be honest about mine… growth is all about stepping out of the shadows, right? I watched a TV show for years and the LORD really convicted me a couple years ago about it. My heart had turned divided over this show because I chose to watch something that *I knew* was not pleasing to the LORD. And by doing this, I had allowed my heart to become calloused to the content of the show over time.

Think of our heart as a fresh apple. When the apple is whole, it is healthy and beautiful. But when we split the apple in half, it doesn't take too long for the apple to turn brown and rot. I don't know about you, but I want a healthy heart, not a rotten one!

Heavenly father, convict me LORD of the ways I have divided my heart against you. Please show me the areas where I have fallen short and have caused me not to love you with all my heart, soul and mind. In Jesus name, Amen.

—Natalie

Today God is stirring my heart by…

BE STILL

"He says, "Be still, and know that I am God."

Psalm 46:10a

Be still. Be still, and know that I am God. Psalm 46:10 is one of the most quoted Bible verses of all time. There are plaques, pillows, t-shirts, large posters to hang on the wall all adorned with this verse. I personally really love this verse.

One morning in particular God used it to speak into me. I was in the middle of my devotions. As I sat there praying, I started to feel overwhelmed with all that was happening in my day. I also started to worry about all that was happening in my life. God lovingly called my name and waited for me to stop. God then reminded me that He cared about what was on my heart. In fact, God cared more about what was on my heart than even I did. He wants change in my life circumstances more than I do. God then whispered to my heart "Be still, and wait on my timing." I was challenged in that moment. I cried out "God, I want to be still. How do I be still when the storm is raging all around me?"

I started to look into this verse a little more to better understand what it means to be still. I loved what I found. The three key phrases that really stood out to where: He says, Be still and Know.

He says. God is the one speaking here. He has all authority over heaven and earth. God's voice is what is breaking through as He addresses the nations. When God speaks, we need to stop and listen.

Be still. According to the NIV Study Bible, the Hebrew for the phrase "Be still" probably means "Enough!" How often does God say this to us? We start to worry, fear or doubt when we are going through a tough time. God doesn't want this for us. He wants us to pay attention to Him. Enough worry and fear. Enough doubt. Enough. Put your eyes back where they belong. I love the Message version of this verse which speaks to this point. "Step out of the traffic! Take a long, loving look at me, your High God, above politics, above everything." We need to Be still and take a long, loving look at God.

The last phrase that stands out to me is Know. To know means to acknowledge. We need to acknowledge in this moment that God is God and He WILL be exalted in all the earth. He will use whatever situations in our life we are going through for His good and His glory. God's mighty acts in our lives point back to Him.

He says, Be still and Know. Three simple but very profound phrases. In what ways do you need to listen to God? What area of your life do you need to be still? What area of your life do you need to acknowledge that God is God and He will take care of you?

Heavenly Father, please teach me to be still and completely trust You. I want to listen when You speak. Teach me what it means to take a long, loving look at You. Instead of doubt or fear, I want to be still before you and trust that You know what you are doing. I want to acknowledge that You are work in my life even when things seem like they are falling apart. Thank You Jesus. I love You, LORD. In Jesus name, Amen.

—Anastasia

Today God is stirring my heart by…

PRAYER IS A POWERFUL GIFT

"I lift up my eyes to the hills—where does my help come from? My help comes from the LORD, the Maker of heaven and earth."

Psalm 121:1–2

As a mother, it is so hard to see your child struggle with life and difficult when we feel that there is nothing we can do about it. My oldest son has been having such a hard time with school this year and it grieves my heart to see him sit at the kitchen table countless times crying because it is so stressful, overwhelming and thinks he can't do it.

One morning when I took him to school with huge tears resting on the brim of his eyelashes, I said, "Just remember all you have to say is 'Jesus help me!' and He will be there!" This was such a good reminder for me also, because as a parent I am not helpless! The creator of the universe is co-parenting with me and has given me such a great gift—prayer. I can intercede for my kids. I can stand in the gap for them. What better love can I show my children than to spend time daily on my knees praying for them. Each morning as I drive my kids to school, I pray out loud over them. These are a few areas I pray about:

I pray over the school and their safety. That God would surround the school with His army of angels and keep all evil out. "The name of the LORD is a strong tower; the righteous run to it and are safe. Proverbs 18:10

I pray over their teachers. That they would be filled with His spirit and that He would pour a blessing over them. "Therefore, as God's chosen people, holy and dearly loved, clothe yourself with compassion, kindness, humility, gentleness and patience." Colossians 3:12

I pray that they are a good friend to others and that they choose good friends. "A friend loves at all times…" Proverbs 17:17. "Do not withhold good from those who deserve it, when it is in your power to act."

I pray over the words they speak. "Put away perversity from your mouth; keep corrupt talk far from your lips." Proverbs 4:24.

I pray over their minds and that they would work hard and try their best. "The sluggard buries his hand in the dish; he will not even bring it back to his mouth." Proverbs 26:15.

I pray for wisdom and that they would make good choices. "I guide you in the way of wisdom and lead you along straight paths. When you walk, your step will not be hampered; when you run, you will not stumble. Hold on to instruction, do not let it go; guard it well, for it is your life." Proverbs 4:11–13.

I pray for help in their time of need. "So do not fear, for I am with you; do not be dismayed, for I am your God. I will strengthen you and help you; I will uphold you with my righteous right hand." Isaiah 41:10

Heavenly Father, thank You for the gift of prayer and that I can come to you whenever and wherever. Nothing is too small or too big of a situation for You. Let me be an great example to my children by showing them what a life saturated in prayer looks like. In Jesus name, Amen.

—Natalie

Today God is stirring my heart by…

SIT DOWN!

"But I trust in you, Lord; I say, "You are my God."

Psalm 31:14

Llamas, horses, pigs, and bunnies. Can you guess where we went this summer? Our kids love going to the 4H fair! They each get to pick an animal they would like to see. We spend the morning going to each animal's barn or area.

When we arrived at the horse barn, Caleb, our 2-year-old, hopped out of the stroller to get a closer look. Then, our 4-year-old Analiah, decided she wanted a turn in the stroller. She's a little too big for the stroller but I didn't mind. I pushed her along for a while. At one point, I turned to look at an animal while pushing the stroller ahead. I felt the stroller jerk to a stop. Analiah had jumped out of the stroller and I had pushed it into her. Oops! I asked her to sit down. Within a minute she was right back in and we moved along.

In, Out, In, Out. The pattern continued. The stress level was also rising within me. I hissed through my teeth "Analiah, please stop getting in and out of the stroller without asking." I explained that she needed to ask before getting out so I didn't run into her. I was so frustrated at her for putting herself in harm's way. Why didn't she just listen to me? Why wouldn't she just sit down? I wanted to save her from being hurt. I am thankful that Analiah finally heard my heart to protect her. The rest of the time she was in the stroller was so much smoother.

In my frustration about this all, I realized that in so many ways, I am a lot like Analiah. I move forward on things without asking. I put myself in harm's way because I feel like I know what's best. Why don't I just listen to God? Why don't I just sit down instead of pushing for my own way? I have a lot to learn too. My Heavenly Daddy really does know what is best for me. I need to trust God's directions, ask for His opinion and then obey. When I do this life is so much easier and filled with a lot less stress.

It amazes me how much God uses my kids to teach me. I guess I shouldn't be surprised. I am very thankful for God's patience with me. How about you? How has God used your children to teach you? Like Analiah and I, do you push for your own way or do you sit down and trust God?

Heavenly Father, I push for my own way too many times. Please teach me to just sit down and trust You. God, You know what is best for me. You don't want to see me hurting. Please help me to listen to You and obey. I want to be a person who surrenders to You. Thanks for Your patience with me. I love You, LORD. In Jesus name, Amen.

—Anastasia

Today God is stirring my heart by…

YOU CAN MAKE A DIFFERENCE

"Therefore everyone who hears these words of mine and puts them into practice is like a wise man who built his house on the rock."

Matthew 7:24

A few years ago, my son Jarrett started playing basketball through a Christian organization called Upward. Bless his heart; the kid didn't have a competitive bone in his body. Like his goal was to not touch the ball. He would usually just stand at half court and dance (I wish I could say it was from the Holy Spirit or his way to thwart the defense, but alas, the boy just loved to move his hips when he got excited). But he was having a great time cheering on his teammates, and that was all that mattered to me! At the beginning of the season, his coach told the team that if they each made three baskets he would take everyone out for ice cream after their last game. Everyone on the team had accomplished this, except my son. So one game day, the coach declared the game "Jarrett's day." The whole team worked together to get Jarrett the ball so he could make his points. Not only did the team cheer him on, but the crowd did as well! To watch my son gain confidence, self-esteem, and make four baskets, brought tears to my eyes.

This is a great reminder for me to remember how he felt that day and how I can make a difference like that in someone else's life. And then I took it a little deeper and began to think about how many times I have missed an opportunity because I wasn't listening to the Lord or spending enough time with Him so He could guide my heart, my words, and my steps. Our relationship with the LORD is very important and our time with Him is about more than just deepening our love and understanding of God, but *furthering* His Kingdom. Just one more reason to remind us that our life is not about us, but our Creator!

Have you taken the time lately to be Jesus to someone? An upward team of second and third graders was Jesus to my son. Are you looking for opportunities or are you head down, focused only on your life? Sadly, I can find myself in that latter category more than I like. Thank goodness for God's saving grace! So join me in taking some time to pray and ask God to lead you to a divine intervention to encourage and make a difference in someone else's life.

Heavenly Father, my desire is to love, serve and honor You. Sometimes that takes me out of my comfort zone, which only goes to show that I can only do things for Your glory and by Your strength. Please guide me LORD so that I can help make a difference today for Your kingdom! In Jesus name, Amen.

—Natalie

Today God is stirring my heart by…

A STEADFAST HEART

"Surely the righteous will never be shaken; they will be remembered forever. They will have no fear of bad news; their hearts aresteadfast, trusting in the LORD."

Psalm 112:6–7

Are you one of those people who likes going to theme parks? Do you love the thrill of the rides and you just can't get enough? There are so many different rides you can go on too. When I was a kid, I remember a ride that spun me around and shook me up. I felt dizzy, sick to my stomach and unstable on my feet. Unless a friend asked me to go, I avoided that ride because I like to be on steady ground.

In life we all have circumstances that can shake us up. The good news is that we don't have to continue to be shaken. How is that possible? What does this look like? How can we receive the worst news and still not be shaken? Through depending on God instead of depending on our circumstances.

Our key verses give some insight in how to walk this out. The psalmist clearly spells out how to never be shaken, remembered forever, and have no fear of bad news. Our heart must be steadfast, trusting in the LORD. What does it mean to be steadfast? The definition of steadfast is fixed in direction; attachment, unwavering, resolution. This is powerful when we look at how this applies to having a steadfast heart and trusting in the LORD. Three key words jump out of these definitions at me—fix, attach, resolve.

First, we need to fix our eyes steadily on Jesus instead of our circumstances. Jesus is the only solid in our lives. In Hebrews 13:8, we read "Jesus Christ is the same yesterday, today and forever." We can depend on Jesus to be consistent. So, when the storms of life come, our focus needs to be on Jesus and not on the storm. Fix your eyes on Jesus alone to have a steadfast heart.

We must also attach ourselves to Jesus in order to have a steadfast heart. What does it mean to attach ourselves to someone? Think about the people you love to spend time with. You clear your schedule to make time to be with them. You do things for the person that are meaningful to them. When we attach ourselves to Jesus, we spend time with Him daily. We clear our schedule to make time to be in His word. We talk to Jesus throughout our day and not just at our devotional time. When you have a steadfast heart, you have attached yourself to Jesus.

And finally in order to have a steadfast heart, we need to resolve. We need to decide to trust Jesus no matter what comes our way. We need to resolve to get down on our knees when the storm is swirling around us. We need to resolve to dig deep in God's word for truth and to receive comfort for whatever we are facing. Resolve to trust Jesus no matter how much our heart is breaking. We need to grab hold of the truth in Romans 8:28 which states "And we know that in all things God works for the good of those who love him, who have been called according to his purpose." God's track record is solid. He will bring good out of any situation because He is God and He is good.

Fix, resolve and attach. Three simple but very powerful words. Will you join me in working these out in your life so you can have a steadfast heart?

Heavenly Father, thank You that I can have a steadfast heart. Thank You that no matter what comes my way, You are there with me. You will fill me with the strength to fix, attach and resolve. You are so good LORD. I love You. In Jesus name, Amen.

—Anastasia

Today God is stirring my heart by...

THE CLAW
OF SIN

"Direct my footsteps according to your word, let no sin rule over me."

Psalm 119:133

One day my family was eating at one of our favorite restaurants and we asked to sit by the games. Our kids are occupied with pretending to play the games while my husband and I get to sit and talk while we wait for the food. It's a win-win situation for all of us, but not for those that actually play the games. One of the games, the stuffed animal grab, is where the claw comes down and you have to pick it up, carry it over to the side and drop it down the slide. I have witnessed *many* people try this game and *never* win. I watch people come up to play and I just want to shout, "Don't do it! You're going to lose. It's not worth it!"

As I watched, I began to see how this machine was an example of my sin. It looks easy, enticing—but I lose every time. Sin is a tricky, sneaky killer. It can grasp its ugly, suffocating, and alluring hold around our hearts and keep us prisoner. Sin has a way of drawing us in and then controlling us, dictating our actions and words. In John 8:34 it says, "Jesus replied, I tell you the truth, everyone who sins is a slave to sin." The sins that get me aren't the huge flashy ones that get people's attention, but the personal, secret ones that seem little, but are just as dangerous.

Satan's easiest job is keeping us enslaved in our sin—because many times, we do most of the work for him. When I lived in Ecuador I would crave food from home and would often sneak down to the mall because they had a KFC or when in the city I'd stop at a McDonald's. Boy did it taste good going down, but hours of regret would follow. You see, about half the time I did this, I would get violently ill or get food poisoning. True story. "Why would you do that?" you ask. I don't know, if I could go back and talk to my 22-year-old self, I would, and then probably inform her about a lot of other things, too.

But why does my 36-year-old self still yell at my kids, lose my patience on a daily basis, allow pride to fill my heart, deal with a selfish spirit? This is what sin does—it looks appealing and yet rots our insides and takes hold of us. We think, "This time it will be different. I can be in this environment, I'm stronger now. I'll stop before it becomes a sin. My sin really isn't all that bad."

What sin is enticing to you? What sin has you in its grasp? The good news is we don't have to be a slave any longer, because Jesus has the power to break us free! He has already paid our price. He has already ransomed Himself in our place. Through Jesus we can have victory.

Heavenly Father, thank You for sending your Son to forgive me for the sin that is keeping me enslaved. In You, death has no sting because You have already paid for my sin. Free me from the sin that entangles me, show me the sin that I don't realize and bring to light the sin I keep hidden so I may draw closer to You. In Jesus name, Amen.

—Natalie

Today God is stirring my heart by…

_____

_____

_____

_____

_____

_____

_____

_____

UNCONDITIONAL LOVE

"The Lord said: "I have loved you with an everlasting love; I have drawn you with unfailing kindness."

Jeremiah 31:3

The text arrives. School is cancelled for today due to the severe weather. Either you are really excited about this fact or you are dreading the day ahead. I would like to say that I am always excited when school is cancelled. But, that is not always the case.

We have had a lot of snow days around here lately. It has made for some crazy days on the home front. I have been trying to be creative with different activities to really embrace and savor the time with my kids. One snow day morning I decided we would lay out the picnic blanket, make some popcorn, drink hot cocoa, and watch a movie together. Sounds so fun, right?

Before implementing my plan and sharing it with the kids, the crazy hour broke out. Every single kid had a behavior issue. There was crying and probably even screaming. Kids were sent to their rooms. You get the picture right? I thought to myself, "Why should I do something so fun and special with my kids when they are acting like this? They are not obeying. Why should I even bother?"

God used that moment to speak into my heart. Deep into my heart. He said to me "Aren't you glad my love isn't conditional?"

It was a holy moment. An "On my knees" in gratefulness kind of moment. Wow! I am so thankful that my God is not a conditional God. I don't deserve anything. But my God choose to give me life by sending His only son to die for me. I don't deserve any special gifts but God chooses to shower me with gifts anyway. I am thankful my God doesn't give me what I deserve. My behavior is not where it should be at times. I don't obey right away. I have my moments of kicking and screaming because I don't understand. But, my God chooses to love me anyway. Just amazing...

After that holy moment in the kitchen, I decided to go through with my plan anyway. I can choose to love on my kids even when they don't obey. I can choose to do fun things for them even if they reject it. I can choose to be like God and love my kids unconditionally. It was a fun morning. It wasn't without other crazy moments but my heart was in a much better place. I am so thankful God spoke into my heart that day.

Aren't you glad God's love is unconditional?

Heavenly Father, thank You for Your unconditional love. I am blown away by it and forever thankful You love me the way You do. Thank you for loving me even when I kick and scream and don't obey You right away. Please help me to love my kids like You love me. In Jesus name, Amen.

—Anastasia

Today God is stirring my heart by...

JESUS KNOWS YOUR PAIN

"Praise be to the God and Father of our LORD Jesus Christ, the Father of compassion and the God of all comfort, who comforts us in all our troubles, so that we can comfort those in any trouble with the comfort we ourselves have received from God. For just as the sufferings of Christ flow over into our lives, so also through Christ our comfort overflows."

2 Corinthians 1:3–5

All of us struggle in life and are given different trials to live and work through, but they are each important and matter to God. The LORD's comfort is not only about making our pain and troubles go away, but also being encouraged, strengthened and given hope to endure those trials and to develop a closer relationship to the LORD. God does not promise an easy and pain free life, but he does promise to love us unconditionally and to always be there for us. We can also be encouraged that we serve not only the one true God, but one that understand ours pain and has experienced some of our very trails. Have you experienced friends or family that have betrayed you or treated you unjustly? Jesus has been there. Have you been wrongly judged? Yep, Jesus has been there. Have you wanted someone to love you so badly, but they won't? Jesus has been there. Have you been rejected? Jesus has been there. Have you lost a loved one? Jesus has been there, too.

I am given great comfort in knowing that when I walk through a storm, God is walking beside me and even carrying me at moments. In John 11:35 it simply says, "Jesus wept." This short and sweet verse is probably one of the most impactful for me in the Bible. It is a reminder that Jesus has also experienced great sorrow in losing someone He loved and understands the heart-wrenching pain we experience. My dad passed away when I was eleven years old and that is a pain and incredible sadness that not many people can understand. I find comfort in knowing God feels my pain, and He doesn't take it lightly.

Whether you are struggling with the loss of a loved one or watching someone you love deal with sickness or a loss, whether you struggle with one of the trails above or something different, find comfort in the truth that Jesus feels and knows your pain. Let Him lead you through this darkness to the light of His love and truth, His power to make the best of your situation so that others may come to know Him, and His hope to remind us that this is not our home.

Heavenly Father, I come before You in thankfulness that You walk alongside me daily. That no hurt, problem, sadness, grief, trail, or loss is bigger than You. Thank You for always being my rock. In Jesus name, Amen.

—Natalie

Today God is stirring my heart by...

_____

_____

_____

_____

_____

_____

_____

_____

PILE YOUR TROUBLES

"Pile your troubles on God's shoulders— he'll carry your load, he'll help you out. He'll never let good people topple into ruin."

Psalm 55:22, MSG

When you hear the word "pile" what picture comes to your mind? It is the piles of laundry that are currently taking over your living room? Or is it the piles of mail that need be gone through? Or maybe the picture that comes to mind might be the pile of groceries that you just came home with or the pile of school papers on your counter that you need to sort through. Piles can be huge or they can be small. In our key verse for today, we are encouraged to take our pile of troubles and place it on God's shoulders. When we do that, there are three things we are promised. Let's take a look.

First, we are promised that God will carry our load. Depending on where you are at in life, your load could feel like a dump truck load of problems. Some of you may even feel like you have a semi-truck filled with troubles. I am not sure what you are facing in life right now, but God knows. And He wants you to pile it on His shoulders. Why? Because God can handle the weight of your problems. You were not intended to carry your problems. God wants you to walk in freedom. Will you pile your problems on God's shoulders today?

Another promise God gives us in this verse is that He will help us out. This blows me away every time I read it. The God that created the whole universe longs to help me. Wow! He cares so deeply about what is going on in my life. God wants to help me by giving me the

313

strength, wisdom and joy that I need. Dear one, God wants to help you too. Will you trust the creator of the world with what is on your heart today? He wants to help you.

And finally, God will not let good people topple in ruin. In the NIV version of this verse, we read that "He will never let the righteous be shaken." What a promise! We live in a fallen world so the circumstances of life are shaky, but we do not have to be shaken when we rest in Jesus. We can take heart and know that Jesus has overcome this world. We have a much better home to look forward to!

God desires us to pile our troubles on His shoulders. He is very capable to carry all of our burdens and all that is on our heart. I can guarantee that your week will go a lot smoother when you pile your troubles on Jesus. Will you let God carry your load, help you out and rest in the promise that God will not let you topple? I hope so!

Heavenly Father, thank You for wanting my troubles. God, will You help me to pile my troubles on You? I don't know why I think I can handle them sometimes. I am not intended to carry these troubles. Thank You for carrying my load. God, I want to let You help me and trust that You will not let me fall. Help me to trust You more. I love You, LORD. In Jesus name, Amen.

—Anastasia

Today God is stirring my heart by…

CLAIM YOUR VICTORY

"In God I trust; I will not be afraid. What can man do to me?"

Psalm 56:11

For me, this verse has more to do with just being afraid, but that all too often we allow the enemy, ourselves, and others to affect our moods, emotions, attitude and self-esteem. Today is a day that we can stand firm in the truth that we are more than conquerors. Let's look at a few areas where we can claim victory!

When we believe the lies, either by what others are telling us or the thoughts controlling our minds… *truth is found in the LORD*— John 16:13a, "But when the Spirit of truth comes, he will guide you into all truth."

When others tear us down by their words or actions… *God lifts us up*—James 4:10, "Humble yourselves before the LORD, and he will lift you up."

When others steal from us… *our riches are found in the LORD*— Colossians 3:24, "Since you know that you will receive an inheritance from the LORD as a reward."

When others hate us… *God loves us*—Romans 8:35a, "Who shall separate us from the love of Christ?" Romans 8:38, "Neither height nor depth, nor anything else in all creation, will be able to separate us from the love of God that is in Christ Jesus our LORD."

When others make us feel alone… *God is always with us*— Hebrews 13:5b, "Never will I leave you; never will I forsake you.")

When others speak negatively of us… *God speaks of us with love, importance, as daughters of the king*—1 John 3:1, "How great is the love the Father has lavished on us, that we should be called children of God." Let that verse soak in for a minute. God, the creator of the universe, wants to lavish His love on you.

So, "What can man do to me?" NOTHING. Why? Because what really matters in life is our salvation. Our salvation comes from the LORD, and no one can take that away from us! Are others weighing you down today? Or maybe you are struggling with how you view yourself? Let me encourage you to find your worth in the LORD. Take hold of His truths. Let Him wrap you up in His loving arms. Allow Him to lift you from the ashes. Today, claim your victory!

Heavenly Father, remind me daily that my victory is found in You! You have overcome the world, so I can stand firm, letting nothing move me because my salvation rest in You. In Jesus name, Amen.

—Natalie

Today God is stirring my heart by…

A STONE BRIDGE

"The LORD says, "I will rescue those who love me. I will protect those who trust in my name."

Psalm 91:14, NLT

"I don't want to!" whined our 3 year old son. No amount of coaxing could get Caleb on the stone bridge. My husband Jonathan was trying to get a picture of all four of our kids on this really cool stone bridge. The bridge was very narrow and about six feet off of the ground.

Do you understand why Caleb didn't want to get on the stone bridge? Honestly, I felt a little nervous myself crossing the narrow bridge. As I watched Caleb, I could see the scare in his eyes. I reminded Caleb that Daddy wouldn't take him where he couldn't protect him. Caleb looked over to Daddy and looked over to the bridge and starting thinking about it.

While Caleb was thinking about it, so was I. The very comment I said to Caleb was one I needed to hear myself. My Heavenly Daddy won't take me where He can't protect me. I was leveled in that moment. God will not take me where He cannot protect me. Even when the bridge is narrow and looks scary to cross or when my heart is breaking in two because of a loss, God will not take me where He cannot protect me.

This past year was filled with many trials. Even when I have an injury that rocked my world, God did not take me where He couldn't protect me. Even when it has been taking a while to heal, God will not take me where He cannot protect me. Even though I had to change my whole eating routine due to food allergies, God did not take me where He was not there to cheer me on and strengthen me.

The same is true for you. When you are asked to step out in faith, God will not take you where He cannot protect you. When you are going through a broken relationship and the hurt is deep, God will not take where you He cannot protect you. When you have lost a child and don't feel like you can take another breath or when your spouse has walked away, God will not take where you He cannot protect you. When one of your best friends moves away, God will not take you where He cannot protect you. When you move away to college and are struggling to make friends or you are a teacher with a really rough class this year, God will not take where you He cannot protect you.

The list goes on and on. Whatever situation you find yourself facing, God will not take where you He cannot protect you. Will you trust your Daddy today and step out onto the stone bridge?

Heavenly Father, thank You that You will not take me where You cannot protect me. As I look back on my life, I see the many, many ways You have been there for me. I see even now the ways You are taking care of me. Thank You for always being a constant in my life. God, please help me to trust You more. I love You, LORD. In Jesus name, Amen.

—Anastasia

Today God is stirring my heart by…

LET'S DANCE!

"And we know that in all things God works for the good of those who love him, who have been called according to his purpose."

Romans 8:28

"Mommy, we are at the BEACH!!" exclaimed my daughter Analiah as she jumped up and down. The wind and ice cold water couldn't dampen her spirit. She wasn't even paying attention to the large waves behind her. She grabbed hold of my hands and started dancing around in circles. The pure joy and innocence was contagious. Soon, I found myself not even thinking about the ice cold water. I couldn't help but smile.

In that moment, I felt so carefree without a care in the world. Shouldn't it always be that way? The creator of the universe is my Daddy. He has everything under control. When the large waves of life come and the ice cold situations happen, why don't I just dance around with joy? Instead, I find myself filled with fear or worry. I question and wonder why I am in this situation. I let the hard times dampen my spirit and take away the joy.

It's in these times that I need to grab my Daddy's hand and dance around. I need to remember that God has been faithful before and He will be faithful again. Like the Psalmist in Psalm 26:3, I can declare "for I have always been mindful of your unfailing love and have lived in reliance on your faithfulness." God's word is filled with verses that speak of His faithfulness. In Psalm 36:5, we read "Your love, Lord, reaches to the heavens, your faithfulness to the skies." God's faithfulness does not end! It reaches past the skies. God is abounding in faithfulness. Psalm 86:15 speaks to this "But you, Lord, are a compassionate and gracious God, slow to anger, abounding in love and faithfulness." God is faithful!

God can calm the large waves of life and warm up the ice cold situations. In Matthew 8:26–27, we read [Jesus] replied, "You of little faith, why are you so afraid?" Then he got up and rebuked the winds and the waves, and it was completely calm. The men were amazed and asked, "What kind of man is this? Even the winds and the waves obey him!" Jesus calmed a pretty major the storm. The disciples stood in awe of His power. Do we trust God to calm our storms? Do we remember and trust that God can use anything for His good?

How about you? Are you letting the hard times damper your spirit? In what ways are you filled with fear or worry? Do you find yourself in a situation that is hard to understand? Will you take your Heavenly Daddy's hand?

Let's dance with our Heavenly Daddy. Let's grab God's hand and twirl around. Let's trust Him to take care of whatever is going on in our life.

Heavenly Father, I am sorry for the ways I have let the hard times damper my spirit and steal my joy. God, I want to trust You more. You have proven Yourself faithful again and again. Help me to take Your hand and dance even when the storms are swirling around me. I love You, LORD. In Jesus name, Amen.

—Anastasia

Today God is stirring my heart by...

WELL DONE, GOOD AND FAITHFUL SERVANT

"Above all, love each other deeply, because love covers over a multitude of sins. Offer hospitality to one another without grumbling. Each one should use whatever gift he has received to serve others, faithfully administering God's grace in its various forms. If anyone speaks, he should do it as one speaking the very words of God. If anyone serves, he should do it with the strength God provides, so that in all things God may be praised through Jesus Christ. To him be the glory and the power for ever and ever. Amen."

1 Peter 4:8–11

God never called us to an easy life, only one that loves and serves Him. He never promised a life without sadness, pain, struggles, or hurt, but He did promise an eternal life free of those. There are times that life is just really hard, and I am in charge of how I handle all the circumstances that come my way. When I'm standing in front of Christ on judgement day, I am only accountable for myself. I won't be standing there with my husband, my children, or my family and friends. So often we can get so consumed over our earthly perspective that we don't grasp what God wants from us. Day in and day out, we should only be focusing on one thing: that when we meet Jesus face to face we hear the words, "Well done, good and faithful servant."

God sees what you are going through. He sees the sacrifices you are making, the right choices you are choosing, and your desire to live a pure life. And I want to encourage you, that God never wastes anything. Even if you never see your harvest here on earth, it will not go void. All the good you are doing will not be in vain. God is preparing a place at His table for you. He is taking into account what you are doing for his Kingdom.

Maybe you are in a marriage where you are giving, loving, serving and respecting, but feel like you are constantly beating your head against a brick wall because you are not getting what you need in return. Keep at it, good and faithful servant. The LORD sees you. Maybe you are constantly serving your children with no recognition or appreciation. Keep at it, good and faithful servant. The LORD sees you. Maybe you are living an honest and pure life, but getting persecuted for it by others. Keep at it, good and faithful servant. The LORD sees you. Maybe it is a battle every day to find the joy in your life, but you refuse to let the enemy take you captive. Keep at it, good and faithful servant. The LORD sees you.

God even encourages us about this in 2 Corinthians 4:16-18, "Therefore we do not lose heart. Though outwardly we are wasting away, yet inwardly we are being renewed day by day. For our light and momentary troubles are achieving for us an eternal glory that far outweighs them all. So we fix our eyes not on what is seen, but on what is unseen. For what is seen is temporary, but what is unseen is eternal."

Heavenly Father, thank You for preparing a home for me with You for eternity. Encourage me in my daily pursuit of following after You to not give up, but to keep pressing forward. In Jesus name, Amen.

—Natalie

Today God is stirring my heart by…

AUTHOR BIO

Natalie Replogle has been a busy stay-at-home mom for the last decade. She has three children and is a wife to her heartthrob, Gregory. She is also the Women's Ministry Director at her church and loves to encourage and help women in their spiritual growth. She enjoys escaping the glamorous life of after-school homework, meal preparation, dirty dishes and laundry by losing herself in writing. She is also the author of the inspirational romance-suspense series, Come to My Rescue. The four book series includes, A Rescued Heart, A Rescued Hope, A Rescued Love, and A Rescued Life. She and her family reside in Northern Indiana. You can connect with Natalie online on Facebook and her blog: www.nataliereplogle.blogspot.com

Anastasia Corbin loves to encourage others in their walk with Jesus. She is crazy about her husband Jonathan. Her superpower is being a Stay at Home Mom of four kids. When Anastasia is not busy saving the day, she loves to hang out with her best friends, sing on Worship team, go for a run or read. Anastasia and her family reside in Northern Indiana. You can connect with her on her website: www.raindropsandhoney.com

Facebook: www.facebook.com/raindropsandhoney
Twitter: @AnastasiaCorbin
Instagram: @AnastasiaMCorbin

ACKNOWLEDGEMENTS

Natalie

Thank you Heavenly Father for placing a desire on my heart years ago to begin writing devotionals for women, and for opening the doors and fulfilling this dream in Your timing. Thank you for continually searching my heart and revealing things in me that are not of You, helping me work through circumstances that strengthen my faith, and for fulfilling my greatest desire of being a mom.

Gregory — I love being on this crazy journey called life with you. I'm thankful daily that you chose me to be your wife and the mother of your children. I wouldn't be where I am today without you by my side and how you love me as Christ loves the Church.

Jarrett, Brayden & Kyla — I am so honored that God handpicked me to be your mom. Many times I look at you and my heart overflows with love, not because you did something great, but just because you are mine. You are each an incredible blessing and fill my life with such joy and happiness. I can't wait to see the plans God has designed for you and I promise to be your biggest cheerleader along the way!

Anastasia Corbin — I am so thankful for your friendship and the opportunity to write this devotional book together. Your passion for Christ is such an inspiration to me. Thank you for being such a prayer warrior for me and for being the friend I know would carry my mat.

MOTTTS (Mothers of Tots to Teens) — Thanks to my group of moms that has turned into family over the last eight years. You are the foundation of this book. I look forward to meeting with you each week as we walk alongside each other, encouraging one another, laughing and crying together, and as you love and support me when I share my faults, struggles, and how God has been working on my heart. You are all incredible moms and I love learning and growing with you.

Thanks to all my family and friends for your support and prayers throughout the process of writing these devotionals. I am blessed and a better person because you are in my life.

Anastasia

Jesus Christ, my Lord and Savior. I would be nothing without you. Thank you for pursuing me so many years ago and literally saving my life. I am forever grateful for your sacrifice. Thank you for filling me with a dream to write. This is all for your glory Lord.

Jonathan, my amazing husband who is my biggest fan. Thank you for believing in me even before I believed in myself. Thank you for loving me so well and cherishing me like a princess. Your countless hours of listening, coaching and praying for me are so appreciated. I love you babe and I am forever yours.

Micaela, Nathan, Analiah and Caleb — You are all an incredible blessing to me in so many ways. I love you all so much! God has poured special giftings into each one of you. I am privileged to have a front row seat to watch God's plan for your life unfold. I commit to growing to be a better Mom for each of you and depending on God to love you even better.

Natalie Replogle — Thank you for believing in me and asking me to coauthor a book with you. I feel so privileged to work with you as I have looked up to as an author and a person long before you asked me. I am blessed to also call you friend. Thank you for your incredible support and prayers through this whole journey.

To the best friends a girl could ask for: Marcie Olson, Tara Rauch, and Kristi Rassi. Thank you for pouring into me, believing in me and encouraging me to pursue my dream of writing. Your countless hours of prayer are also a huge blessing.

Aimee Weishaupt — thank you for your incredible support in watching my younger kids so I can have uninterrupted times to write. Thank also for encouraging the gift of writing you saw in me and for your amazing prayer support.

Jewel Sawatsky, my mentor Mom, who has poured into in countless ways. Thank you for loving me and encouraging me to be more like Jesus.

Keri Smart — thank you for your encouragement and help with the kids at times so I could write. Thanks for cheering me on and listening so well.

There are so many friends who have prayed for me as I wrote this book. I know there are many more than I have listed here but I do want to thank Janette Griffith, Kim Landes for helping with the kids, my sister Beth, Amber Miller, Lael Nafziger, Jenny Yordy, Mindy Miller, Jan Longcor, my adopted Mom and Dad – Scott and Sarah Yoder, and my amazing small group (Ken and Sara Hochstetler, Matt and Joanna Yordy, Tommy and Tammy Simpson, and Christi and Cory Havens) Love you all!

Lael Nafziger Photography, for the amazing talent in my author and blog pictures.

To my Facebook friends- thank you for the countless FB comments of encouragement as I shared my writing. Thanks for believing in me!

Natalie and Anastasia Would Like to Thank...

White Feather Press — Skip and Sara, thank you for believing in us and our desire to reach out to other moms and encourage them to turn to God when their bases are loaded. Without you, this dream wouldn't be possible.

Darcy Holsopple Photography — Thank you so much for your servant's heart and going above and beyond to take pictures for the book cover out of the goodness that overflows from your heart. Not only are you a very talented photographer, but also a woman whose love for Jesus radiates.

Ron Bell — We are deeply thankful and appreciate all your hard work and flexibility as we worked on producing the vision for the cover. You knocked it out of the park!

Nick Mulder — Thanks for enduring editing a moms devotional book. We are sure you learned way more than you wanted to about the life of women and moms. You're a good man.

A Rescued Heart:

Kindergarten teacher Ava Williams' life is forever changed when her groom never shows up for the wedding, leaving her heartbroken and entangled by the rejection and lies. SWAT officer Matthew Thompson lives for saving and protecting others, but can he rescue Ava from herself? Ava attempts to help a student's mom break free from domestic abuse, but things become complicated when she is caught up in the tragedy when an irreversible decision causes a backlash of chaotic events.

A Rescued Hope:

Ava Williams finds herself the target of a dangerous man with a corrupt past, while the city of Rockford is experiencing an outbreak of drug use. SWAT officer Matthew Thompson is working on both cases and begins to piece together that the cases just might have a common thread. Derek Brown and Julia Anderson's paths have finally crossed - and what a collision it has caused. Friendship becomes their foundation with a tease of something more. Can they work through their pasts before it's too late to salvage a future?

A Rescued Love:

Julia Anderson is caught in the middle of a situation that leads to murder, and she is the only eye-witness. When strange occurrences begin to happen in the aftermath, SWAT officer Derek Brown takes her to his family's cabin to keep her safe until they can figure out what is going on with the case that has taken a sudden change of events. As Julia deals with a secret she has revealed, Derek must face his family and their different views on how he should live his life. Can they learn to work together through their trials or will it tear them apart forever?

A Rescued Life: Coming soon!

Chef and rising artist, Lucy Williams, has found herself in uncharted circumstances as a suspect in a murder investigation. Detective Trevor Hudson prides himself on not allowing cases to cross over from professional to personal, until he meets the flighty-spitfire, Lucy Williams. As Trevor and Lucy work together, the case takes many twists and turns and becomes more dangerous than either of them imagined - for their safety and their hearts. Secrets are uncovered and feelings begin to change and deepen as they search for the truth that will hopefully set them both free.

57429884R00183

Made in the USA
Charleston, SC
12 June 2016